1

Risk Management for
Consumer Price Protection

The concepts developed in this book are extracted from
two published patents by the official Gazette of United
States Patent and Trademark Office, awarded to the author
in 2011and 2012.

Published by CreateSpace Independent Publishing Platform,
North Charleston, SC, USA

ISBN-13: 978-1523628346 (CreateSpace-Assigned)
ISBN-10: 1523628340

Library of Congress Control Number: 2016903241

Risk Management
for
Consumer Price Protection

An Overview

The business of derivatives has significantly evolved since the late 90's, mainly due to electronic trading platforms which has made it possible to trade many products, rather than limited traditional contracts. The industry now enjoys global recognition as an important contributor to capital markets where buyers and sellers trade "legally binding" derivatives to make or take delivery of specific goods at an agreed time and place. The price, as a variable, is continually discovered through an auction-like process. This "discovery" is made by changes occurring in supply (seller) and demand(buyer). The marketplace then disseminates such information to public on instantaneously. For an efficient market there must be a buyer for a seller during a given session. This property of instant availability of trader is the measure of liquidity. Hedging is an offsetting vehicle used by a trader against the risks associated with price changes in the market. Prior to introduction of electronic exchanges, the old auction forum took place by an "outcry" in an open physical space[1], whereby the floor brokers would *cry* their price as bid or offer; the first matched bid and offer would be the last executed trade, displayed on a large billboard. The US commodity exchanges trade limited standardized items, ranging from agricultural to industrial and energy. These products are mainly primary level of manufacturing. For example gold contract specifies a gold bar with exact dimensions and weight. Since the 1980's the financial and energy product continue to dominate the marketplace because of significant demand. The introduction of swaps as semi- standard form of contracts now permit the exchanges to trade and clear almost any products. This has also created unintended consequences that in the past resulted in significant financial losses.

The so called over-the-counter products(OTC), dominated by customized contracts, have expanded dramatically, and in particular, in the financial sector. Derivatives contracts, or essentially semi-standard or non-standard products were pioneered by energy traders many years ago. The most popular form of such contracts (swaps) make it possible for producer and or consumer of goods to transfer their risk to a dealer. The risk takers, in turn, pass on their risk via an established derivatives market. Such products trade as forward contract, the price of which swings within a range between "floor" and "ceiling". In transactions handled as swaps the risk is basically "controlled" by a dealer; the large commercial banks are major beneficiaries. If on the other hand, the transaction takes the course of formal exchanges the dealer will absolve himself from any risk and the investment banks as market makers benefit most. This is based on the process financial clearing. The existing exchanges are accordingly the most likely candidate to perform in-house clearing. The examples are Chicago Mercantile Exchange(CME) which trades agricultural, energy and financial futures and Intercontinental Exchange (ICE) dominating swaps market in energy and recently[1a].

The cycle of trading a product comprises three key elements. First, a marketplace for exchanging information that may be a physical location where buyer and seller meet or an electronic platform where buyers and sellers interact through electronic medium. The second element is a list of financial instruments[1b] that are tradable in the market. The third component is a process to give an executed trade crediblity and certainty. This particular component itself involves several distinct functions that are collectively known as clearing of trade; the closing of the trade cycle is then called settlement.

There are, of course, additional and necessary functions that are essential to the entire trading platform. The most significant ones are cash management, risk management, logistics or delivery of goods as well as dissemination of information containing market data and news[1c].

Some or all of these functions may be integrated into a single trading platform. The level of integration itself may be highly localized or may have certain degree of flexibility to communicate beyond its geographical borders. As an example CME has an interconnectivity for virtual clearing with Singapore Exchange for selective financial products. ICE, on the other hand, operates an electronic trading platform dedicated to energy and food products as well its recently acquired NYSE that exclusive-ly trades equities all as standalone operation.There is no interconnectivity or integration in this exchange. International markets are even less equipped to interconnectivity or integration.

The hybrid trading platform (HTP) is a single electronic trading platform[1d] (Node) that contains the properties of seamless integration, product independent and interconnectivity to allow multiple trading locations all having access to live matching complete with self clearing capability and payment system. A typical Node is tailored to trade both standard and semi-standard products serving local products and services. An open clearing environment allows traders to access open books. It allows open contracts be matched and cleared electronically between any two Nodes. The new marketplace accommodates trading of large number of products used in non traditional businesses in manufacturing sectors as well as IT industry.

In chapter the basic philosophy of hybrid trading electronic platform is outlined. The HTP comprises flexible multi-level trading of cash market, complete physical delivery and forward contracts to utilize the principles of risk management while maintaining sufficient flexibility to behave as forwards. The main characteristics of HTP as compared to various conventional platforms are detailed in Table 2.

This book is organized in four parts. Part one (chapter II, chapter III and chapter IV) deals with the design and operation of a standalone trading platform as a Node. Part two is devoted to chapter V dealing with interconnectivity at national and international level with the necessary flexibility and autonomy based on local or regional conditions. Part three identifies two special applications of HTP in manufacturing and retail business to demonstrate how the principle of risk management can provide price protection for end users(or consumers) particularly in volatile and unpredictable environment. Two separate industries, electronics manufacturers and energy consumptions are separately discussed in chapter VI and VII. Part four contains chapters VIII, IX and X. The materials covered in these chapters are tools that were applied to important issue of improving liquidity by analyzing and enhancing the bid and ask process and narrowing the spreads. Additional tools for non financial applications are offered; for example, streamlining the auction process in chapter IX. In chapter X, new steps are explored which include generation of market data and news affecting supply and demand for products with further enhancement of analytical tools.

Chapter II describes the essence of a Node as the efficient method by extending risk management for various contracts across the trading platform without the required conditions or use of intermediaries to enter different marketplaces. In so doing, a trader can conveniently hedge a position against spot as he trades forwards. He is also able to do the same against calendar based deliveries. The heart of a trading platform (Node) is the listed products offered for trade. The selection and subsequent designing of products is detailed in chapter III. In this chapter, the principles of the process is detailed below.

- Technical identification of the physical product
- Market intelligence as related to the product group.
- Market intelligence as related to suppliers and consumers.

The principles outlined here prepares the ground for a convenient and systematic means for developing any non-traditional contracts.

The HTP is a fully integrated end-to-end system. Beyond the order processing, three main components are employed to perform this task. Chapter IV describes the essential components of cash management module, the settlement including the physical delivery module all treated as one monolithic unit. This unit contains cash market operation for derivatives, as well as non-derivative tradable products such as equities and financial products at local or regional or national levels.

Chapter V discuss the interconnectivity issues involved in creating a inter-networked trading platform. Trading centers, or Nodes are autonomous, but they are interconnected. Matching takes place globally as if there is one node. All settlements take place at the Node where the match has taken place.

The next two chapters VI and VII are devoted to applications of HTP in manufacturing and retail sectors. The business model provides a mechanism which guarantees price as well as availability of in-process-materials for manufacturers. The manufactured products in electronics and energy are introduced to demonstrate how risk management can be a powerful tool for stabilizing and hence protecting prices for manufacturer, distributors, aggregators and ultimately consumers.

For retail market Hybrid Trading Platform is utilized to trade swaps with built-in risk protection mechanism, allowing retailers as well as end user (consumer) to protect their buying power. Dealer manages his risk by directly using HTP calendar month contract or the conventional futures platform using conventional options platform.

The purpose for demonstrating the application of HTP in retail business is to stress the basic advantage of risk management in terms of price transparency as a powerful tool for protecting consumers as well as quantifying of value-add. The commonly known term of consumer protection is presently thought of legal protection. Generally, a set of laws are designed to protect the rights of consumers against noncompetitive markets or market fraud.

These complex legal cases, usually, involve a class of people, resulting in lengthy and expensive endeavor that sometime serves political objectives. In truth, ordinary consumers do not have the means or the time to "discover" the true price of goods. In order for markets to offer their goods at fair price is for distributor to be aware of the *true* price. The pharmaceutic-al products would be a good example. The key is to develop open market for non-patented medical products which enjoy a significant consumptions. Creation of spot(cash) market will lead to price discovery in recognized exchanges similar to gasoline, coffee and corn.

The advanced order matching described in chapter VIII employs some simple techniques that assist the traders to develop additional parameters as matching criteria, thereby improving liquidity. One matching criterion may be assumed to be an increased "potential number of matches". This is a new element that improves the process of standard order matching, based on bid or offer, where price alone would limit the number of matches leading to unrealistic spread.

Chapter IX is devoted to enhancements that can be made towards the existing one-to-many auction houses by automating the key ingredients towards achieving straight through processing.

The financial industry in recent years has helped create a sophisticated cottage industry known as data vendors who basically disseminate the market data generated by the exchanges. Their less visible role, however, is more critical. Their generation of news based on the analysis of retrieved data, when used as feedback to capital market, could instantly move large amount of funds as gain or loss to someone. These soft data can be filtered, manipulated and sometime biased. Except the energy and agricultural businesses most traditional producers are not able to effectively manage their production and marketing, because the market data needed to assess the demand for their products to adjust their supply as well as prices is hard to come by. The key is the introduction of new manufactured products traded in a Node allowing the market data to become available for dissemination. The goal of chapter X is then to outline a technology-driven analytical system which identifies, monitors and measures risk elements in manufacturing environment in real time. The system integrates financial, accounting and marketing disciplines.

Finally, to enable the corporate management to seamlessly adjust its project-ed cost of goods sold into real-time value, based on movement in the cost of material component. A proprietary methodology for Product Identification (PI) automatically classifies the products of a producer and index that in terms of "value-added". The measuring (versus directional) technique includes standard indexing and quantitative analysis with discrete models that can be simulated repeatedly. A quantitative financial analysis will then adjust company's projected key financial data.

TABLE OF CONTENT

PART FOUR

PART ONE

Chapter I
A Hybrid Trading Platform (HTP)

Introduction

The HTP is a flexible trading platform for any asset class of products with built-in clearing system including cash management, matching engine, risk management tools and physical delivery module.

The abstract diagram(Fig.1) shows how a marketplace with market makers can generate liquidity in a hybrid, forward and futures trading platform, applying risk management tools. HTP has the following features;

- built-in liquidity generator with flexible, semi custom design contract.
- dealer to trader interface or interaction in the same platform.
- convergence of structured and unstructured contracts
- a single platform marketplace for cash, cash forward and calendar month.

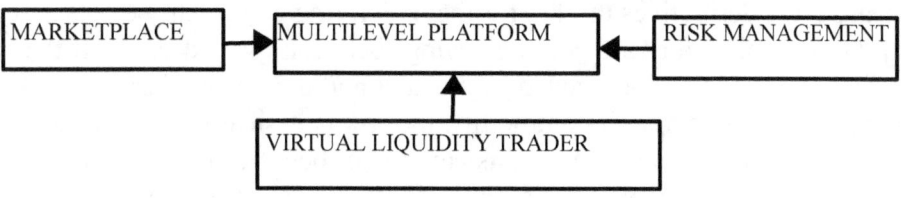

Fig 1: an abstract view

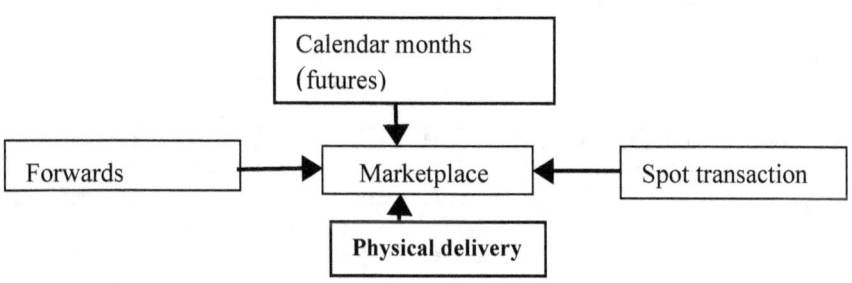

Fig 2. multi-level trading

In recent years the over-the-counter market, dominated by customized agreements (contract), has expanded dramatically and in particular, in the financial sector. The most popular form of contracts traded are swaps making it possible for producer and or consumer of goods to transfer their risk to risk takers through a dealer. Dealers are able to pass on their risk because the derivatives market for the underlying commodity exists and is liquid. A typical forward contract swings between two extremes. If the transaction is handled as a swap by a dealer and there is no derivative market for the underlying commodity, the risk is basically transferred to the dealer and the commercial banks are major beneficiary. If on the other hand, the transaction takes the course of formal exchanges dealer will absolve himself from any risk and the investment banks benefit most.Financial instruments are commonly "products" ranging from simple forwards to more complex futures and options. The progression as compared to HTP is tabulated below.

Table 1: Comparing HTP to other trading models

Financial instrument elements	Forwards, unstructured	Swaps, unstructured	Futures, structured	Hybrid Platform
delivery	Any agreed date	Fixed dates	Fixed calendar month(s)	30,60 , 90 day multiple. of 90
quantity	any	Flexible	Fixed lot	adjustable lot
price	Agreed bilaterally	Fixed one side, dealer float	float	float
Clearing	Private	Private	Local exchange or via central clearinghouse	distributed clearing escrow a/c
settlement	usually physical except currencies and interest rates	Physical and cash	Usually cash through a financial institution.	Physical & cash offset / local banks
Risk Management	1.Both parties assume risk on agreed date and price. 2.Either party may hedge position against underlying commodity	1.Dealer assumes risk on agreed date and price. 2. Dealer may hedge position against underlying commodity.	1.Performance bond 2. Daily marked-to-market pricing based on Fixed delivery dates	Perf. Bond. Daily mark to market pricing based on 26 weeks delivery.
Contract design	Custom	Usually Custom	standardized	Semi custom
Product spec	any	flexible	standardized	Standard root product
Transaction party	bilateral	Bi-lateral thru dealer	multilateral	Multi lateral
Physical warehouse	Bilateral arrangement	Bilateral arrangement	Fixed designated location	Global bond warehouses

As the table indicates a financial instrument contains certain characteristics. Depending on the degree of trading sophistication, a trading mode ranges from most risk exposed to best risk managed. The marketplace is most liquid in a structured marketplace, but the products that can be so designed are limited to largely financial industry and industries such as traditional commodity market. Most forward contracts in almost all non financial sectors are therefore exposed to risk either by parties involved or by dealers (in case of swaps). The Hybrid Trading Platform introduces methodologies by which an extended class of products can be developed that would behave as financial instruments. These new products will be flexible to accommodate changes taking place in production, technology, environmental and life cycle. Similarly the governing financial instrument's contract will be flexible to accommodate different products. Chapter III is devoted to this topic. There are three key components that define the essence of the Hybrid Trading Platform as an integrated exchange.

Order matching process
The Trading session is generally based on certain rules that define the beginning and end of session. In a classical form the complete trade cycle consists of pre trade which includes price inquiry; order routing and execution and finally post trade that settles the account. Usually orders, consisting of bids and offers are routed to specific marketplace where the product is traded, the contract with the expected degree of liquidity. The period of trade is flexible and could change at any time depending on matching. The orders are received on random basis if the marketplace is closed, but it will be time stamped during the time that marketplace is open. The US markets are grouped as equities, bonds or commodities; all well established marketplaces and principally just a few. As a result, the trading procedure are highly centralized and therefore compartmentalized.

The most important element of trading is the matching engine owned and protected by the marketplaces. This black box controls the entire trade. Matching is based on price, lot quantity and delivery time. The matching engine generates the following results.

- Best Price (not least) discovered
- Matched orders are cleared instantly
- Orders are Settled daily
- Real time order status

If no match takes place the order remains in the "bin" for the next cycle or session. The frequency of session depends on the number of matched orders. As the market becomes more liquid the frequency of session approaches a continuous-like matching session.

The unmatched order is retained until the end of the business day and then discarded unless the order type is good to cancel (GTC). In case a match is found by the end of the business day, the user is notified by email about the match. The user can also check orders on screen at any time to see the status. Unmatched orders can be cancelled at any time. In chapter VIII advanced methods for matching is discussed.

Separate modules such as cash management and physical delivery will provide a seamless integration as one-stop shop service for participants. Chapter IV shows how these modules would accommodate Straight Through Processing.

Risk management
The most important element of the HTP trading platform is its built-in risk management feature that would significantly contribute to its liquidity. The following table 2 describes the relevant definitions and terms.

Definitions
Table 2-Terms and references

Mark(ed)-to-market	cash trader's maintenance margin account is updated. It measures the extent of risk
Spot Market	Goods, at any quantity, are delivered upon purchase
Cash market and cash forward/swap	Only cash is being used as a medium of transaction. Cash "contract" is sale agreement for immediate delivery or
Margin and maintenance margin	The amount needed to trade. To maintain this deposit against price movement for short term period.
Integrated clearing	Clearing of matched orders and settlement of accounts at a specified time within the system
Offset	Taking an opposite and equal position usually in form of ca
CLOB	Centralized limit order booking (aggregated from all trading centers)

Risk management essentials

Generally risks are typified as speculative or inherent; they are either static or dynamic. Risk management is a tool for removing the lack of knowledge about the type of risk.Risk management is a tool for removing the lack of knowledge about the type of risk. Risk is normally reduced or avoided by shifting it from, say, consumer to risk taker. The two major risks in business are price and liquidity.

Risk management essentials are typified as speculative or inherent; they are either static or dynamic. Risk is normally reduced or avoided by shifting it from , say, consumer to risk taker. The two major risks in business are price and liquidity.

Market Risks generally include price, interest rate and currency exchange rates. Any movement in such variables will be undesirable to the market participants.

The Liquidity Risks are sharply reduced in recent years credited to financial markets' innovations. Energy and some basic manufactured products such as steel and pulp are now "commoditized" and others will surly follow.

The Credit Risks generally refer to participant's default and credit quality transitions for a transaction. In a given sector, say, manufacturing the lack of diversity may produce systemic risk. As the number of participants, in a trading forum, increases the Credit Risk is reduced because fewer traders will default and credit risk is less likely.

The services for risk management and related issues are listed below.
- Pure financial risk management
- Pure physical risk management
- Full service risk management

Performance bond is generally required as collateral, margins and margin maintenance in trading and financial markets. Probably the simplest of credit risk protection is performance bond that, depending on credit worthiness of the participant, may vary greatly from a few percent to one-hundred percent all in cash or cash equivalent such as US Treasury. In the case of traders who take large positions or are well established, a performance bond in non-cash form such as letters of credit would be accepted in lieu of cash. performance bond may be fixed, or static, for the entire contract period as it is customary in construction contracts, or it may

19

be dynamic as practiced in financial trading arena. In this case the term margin replaces performance bond. In order to update its value, based on a new price. The term, maintenance margin is used to determine the frequency and the amount at which a new margin is established. The purpose is to minimize the marketplace's exposure associated with wide price fluctuations. This procedure is known as mark-to-market, or marked -to-market.

SWAPS explained

The principle of swaps is the same as forwards. Dealers fix the price of an instrument at one end of a trade, e.g., buyer and try to manage the risk of price change at the other end of the trade who is the seller. A dealer who has fixed the price with the buyer at one end then "floats" the price with a seller at the other end. Depending on the direction the price may move (during the life of contract) at each time the dealer will give or receive "compensation". This price deviation is, sometime, within a range which is agreed between the parties; in practice this is regulated by official financial agencies such as futures trading or unregulated derivatives such as default swaps. The key here is the instrument of risk transfer from the buyer(or seller) to a dealer.

In the energy business, for example, it is the underlying commodity that is traded in a liquid market. Forward contracts generally may or may not be tied to underlying commodities traded in the same market. If the underlying commodity is traded as a financial instrument dealers are able to take advantage of built-in risk transfer mechanism. The dealer, in this case simply computes the equivalent contract needed for the underlying commodity to hedge his position. Such risk management makes it possible for dealer to perform swap without involving counter-party by either offsetting internally or hedging externally.

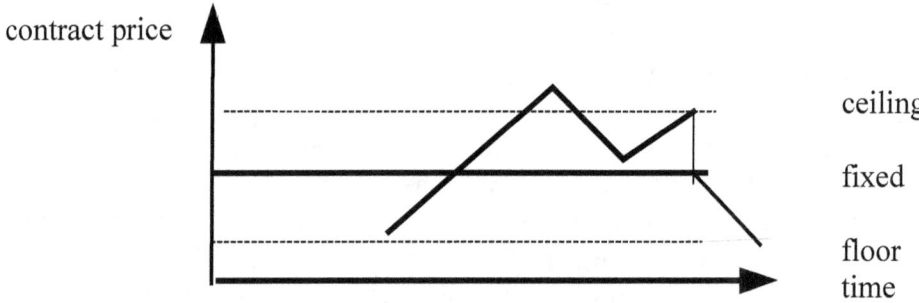

Fig. 3: a physical swap contract between one party of trade and a dealer.

20

Trading party contract price

Ultimately, dealer may have to find a way to hedge his position if the price exceeds the expected range. Normally, the swaps are long term contracts during that time the short term price gyration may be minimal. Dealers are also able to take simultaneous positions by being a buyer against a producer and seller to a consumer, assuming there is a match between buyer and seller. Under each scenario a separate agreement is drawn and dealer will receive or compensate both parties. The only risk, here, is the credit risk to which the dealer may be exposed.

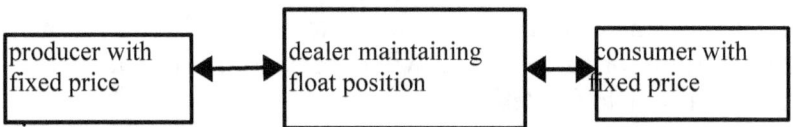

Fig 4: transaction flow between dealer and both buyer and seller

Principals of mark-to-market

- Mark-to-market (M-to-M) is an accounting method as opposed to accrual method where revenue is recognized when goods are delivered.
- Marketer generally is a producer who hedges his position against eventual physical delivery and therefore need not be concerned with M-to-M.
- Trader in contrast is not interested in delivery so he needs to use M-to-M.
- Some physical contracts are structured to allow settlement without delivery, where M-to-M becomes necessary.
- Contract's financial aspect of risk refers to price while the physical risk refers to delivery.
- Replacement cost, or liquidation damage, D= contract value - market value, price compensation to avoid punitive damage.
- A number of valuation factors are required for calculating M-to-M, notably:

Forward curves for the underlying commodity may be used to determine the price criterion. In absence of such data extensive development of market intelligence, current economic and market condition will be needed.

The curve is based on brokers and or dealers bid and offer. It will be then necessary to compare contract price with absolute market price mid-point.

- Time value of money (interest rate related).
- Traded currency.
- Counter party credit risk which similar to bad debt.

Procedure for calculating mark(ed)-to-market

The contracts move in forwards fashion which means every day the contract and its delivery date move. The mark–to-market requires a fixed date against which a price measurement becomes applicable. One way to do so is to designate arbitrary calendar dates. On each calendar date delivery, certain forward contract will expire, both before and after, as user's reference date for delivery.

- Fix 26 periods (every 15 days calendar-wise).
- Allow user to pick a date.
- Date will coincide with either prior or next fixed date depending on its proximity.

The mark-to market will then be measured against the nearest calendar date to the given contract.

Example

Delivery dates for fixed periods are set at first and 15th of calendar months. October 1, October 15, November 1, November 15, .etc.

On October 2, user may select an arbitrary date, say, October 22, for which the expiry date will assume October 15 because it is farthest to November 1. Hence the M-to-M price of October 15 will be the reference.

Alternatively, a user who selects a 30 day contract on October 2, his expiry date is automatically November 1.

Table 3: Flexible delivery schedule fitted in fixed 30, 60 and 90 day contract

Swap Trade period	Oct.15	Nov1	Nov.15	Dec. 1	Dec.15	Jan 1
Contract	30day	60 day	60 day	90 day	90 day	
Sept 15-25	Contract delivery					
		Contract delivery	Contract delivery			
				Contract delivery	Contract delivery	

Liquidity improvement

Market based multilateral netting, fulfills almost all requirements needed for liquidity especially for less liquid market. Specifically, it provides credit anonymity and removes credit risk from the industry. In a liquid market contracts frequently change hands by market makers who are the key liquidity creators; and not the producers and consumers.

The modern market makers are now replaced by "high frequency" traders, as the trading arena has decided shifted from "outcry" in a physical pit to electronic marketplace trading platform. The liquidity is even more critical because of much faster speed of price change from ticker tape to computer screen.

The greatest achievement in improving the liquidity of a physical good is to free producer or supplier from commitment to holding contract until the goods are delivered at the promised date. The technique that allows the physical good be transformed to a financial instrument, i.e., a tradable contract is typically classified as securitization.

The primary market in some businesses such as equipment manufacturers, e.g., consumer product lacks any liquidity because it has no secondary market to allow risk transfer take place. To understand this phenomenon it is helpful to remind readers that crude oil -and later natural gas- as two important consumer products was introduced to commodity market in 1981.

Prior to that crude oil pricing was fixed by major international oil companies, based on Mexican gulf and Persian gulf benchmarks. There was no secondary market because all crude oils were sold by the marketers to refiners. The secondary market was not developed either by the producer of crude nor the refiner. In fact the commodity exchange people established contracts as financial instruments based on information that had become available through initially Dutch shipping ports. Traders were able to act as market makers by trading crude oil carried by tankers free on board.

This was the first step towards creation of liquidity for the underlying commodity. An "internal" intermediary had assumed the role of a "liquidity trader" which was the first step, necessary to create a secondary market. Such intermediary required a pricing advantage from the so-called information trader who is merely interested in making a purchase, on the buyer side, or to sell his goods.

The market maker is thus a liquidity trader who makes it possible for marketers or hedgers to take advantage of transferring their risk. The central issue, here, is a favorable forward price that would give incentive to market maker. This translates to a price spread which is the difference created between the two sides of the trade, known as bid and offer. A market maker is attracted by small and equitable risk associated with the spread. An "information trader" is then needed to monitor inventory position of rapid price change as well as price continuity.To create such environment an advanced trade execution system is developed that operates as a "trade assisted" market maker. Refer to Fig.5 and Fig.6.

Table 4: Comparing derivatives trading platforms

Derivatives	Contracts type	Liquidity quality	Transaction cost
Forwards	Flexible, Bi-lateral	Contingent on collateral or credit	high
Futures & options	Standardized and fixed, Multilateral	Cash and or letter of credit	medium
Hybrid trading platform	Standard root & semi-standard Multilateral	All the above	low

Expanding the marketplace participants
The traditional marketplaces' participants such as manufacturer as producer of root or basic materials, e.g., silicon in electronics and continuous processes of value adders of new products as well as other users, for example, consumers as distributors are basically "information" trader.

To enlarge the size of participants it is essential to provide a single platform for many products, all derivatives and all available delivery schedules

- The underlying traded commodity, as financial instrument, will encourage swap dealers, for hedging purpose, to participate in a single platform marketplace.
- Spot and forward contracts are traded on single platform will be convenient for hedgers.
- Single pricing is established for institutions and retail market; hence attracting retailers.
- Multi trading facilities are networked to accommodate local day traders and investors (speculators). The information sharing capability among all facilities will bring information trader and market makers to close proximity. In this fashion rapid price adjustments as well as price uniformity will take place.

- Trading in local currencies (of trading facility) would allow products to be traded in an already liquid (currency) market. This will attract currency traders.

Improved efficiency through advanced matching

The efficiency of open cry pit with respect to price discovery is superior to standard electronic matching. The problem of sequencing of orders commonly utilized in electronic matching may be offset against concurrent bid and ask in an open cry pit as follows.

- Monitoring AND FLAGGING "inventory" position of limit orders, for example, large limit buy or small limit sell indicating upward price trend.

- Containing the match by designating a relatively small lot quantity

- Aggregate limit orders (centralized booking). Implementing centralized limit order. Such system, also known as Consolidated Limit Order Book, displays all limit orders in a centralized fashion. Centralizing a limit order book allows an aggregation of all limit orders to be available for automatic matching.

- Specified price range associated with limit order. Limit order with price range can be provided by participant. Improvement will be made if ranges are defined by buyer and seller. the system limit order will have an attached "specified price range, i.e, buying if price is $X(1+y\%)$ or sell at $X(1-y\%)$. This kind of marketing information is particularly applicable to corporate participants. Refer to Fig. 8

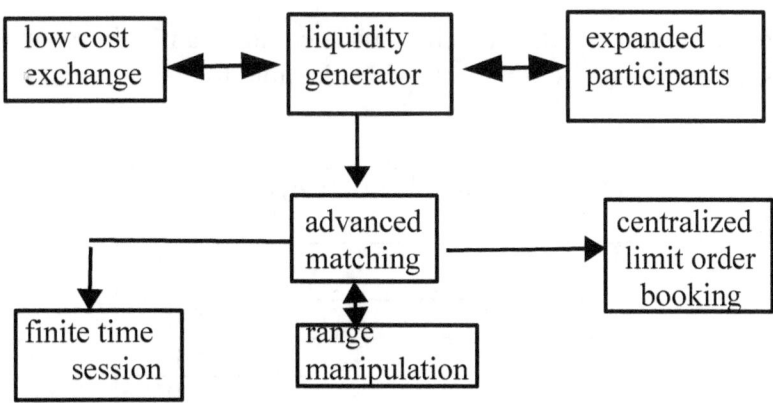

Fig.5. liquidity generator/trader

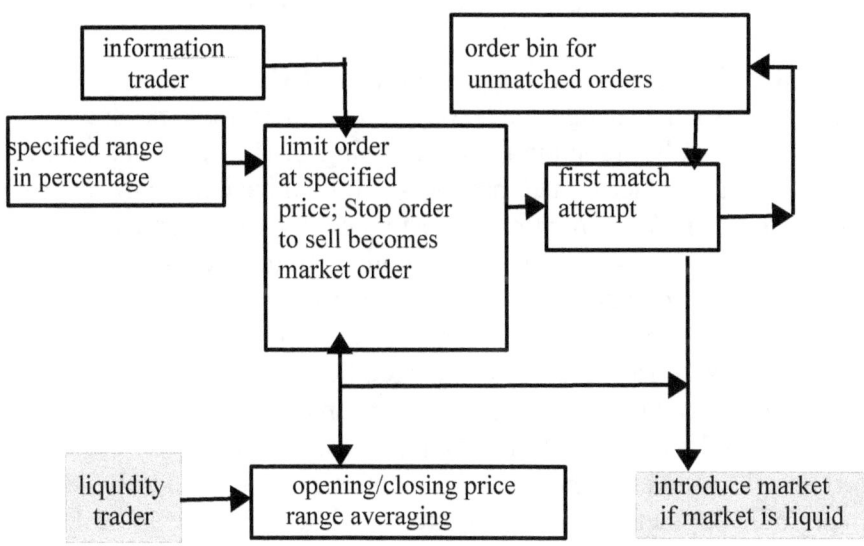

Fig. 6: virtual market maker

Discovering price based on price matching for a finite time
Limit orders generally are indicative of the range of price as per recent transactions. Averaging last cleared prices is X. The next bid is X-d1,... and the next offer is X+d'1...

Period of session in which a match id made could be any T in seconds or minutes depending on liquidity rate. For example for T=25 second:

Table 5

Number of orders	Bidding	number of orders	Asking
2	5.00	1	5.05
1	4.98	3	5.02
4	4.97	4	5.04
5	4.98	6	5.01

The standard approach is to draw supply and demand curves to locate the intersection point; hence the matching price. The matched orders are timed as First In First Out(FIFO). Improvement will be made if the range is narrowed where buyer and seller can quickly converge.

Convergence of off-exchange marketplaces and HTP
Trading houses, such as hedge funds, buy and sell derivative products which are not normally traded in formal exchanges. They are considered off-exchange marketplaces. Such products will then have to be treated as forwards. The risk management mechanism, here, will of course have to be devised differently, usually by trading houses' traders individually. Common type is for one party to a trade to enter into a separate agreement with third party to insure the performance of the counter-party. In this manner the particular risk is being exchanged between the counter-party and, say, a swap provider or dealer. The arrangement between swap provider and party "A" stipulates that in case of default by party "B" the party A will receive a contingent payment from swap dealer while certain periodic payment as credit premium will be sent to swap dealer by party A. The two parties may then agree on a "netting" arrangement in case of default. The HTP applies standard performance bond as primary risk management tool, but the exact amount of that may be flexible based on credit quality of participant. A more advanced tool known as mark-to

-market is also employ-ed, the pricing of which is based on spot averages plus the relevant interest rate. More detailed explanation is given in chapter II.

The quality of liquidity, in a trading house ranges from liquid (cash) to contingent (collateral & letter of credit), to financing. In the case of financing, the source and its use is generally treated as off- balance- sheet. In the HTP both cash and domestic letter of credit will be used.

Interfacing dealer with trader
In an OTC marketplace dealer fixes price on one end while assuming the risk on the " floating" side. Dealer would want to protect himself against unexpected price changes. Two possible scenarios are shown in the following tables 10 and 11.

- If underlying commodity is already traded and liquidity is established, dealer interchanges position with trader through an established exchange.
- If the open market for underlying commodity is not available HTP acts as a single platform where dealer and trader are interchangeable. The HTP platform has built-in risk management tools allowing dealer to hedge his position. The HTP offers, in effect, a contract that behaves as both forwards(swaps) and futures.

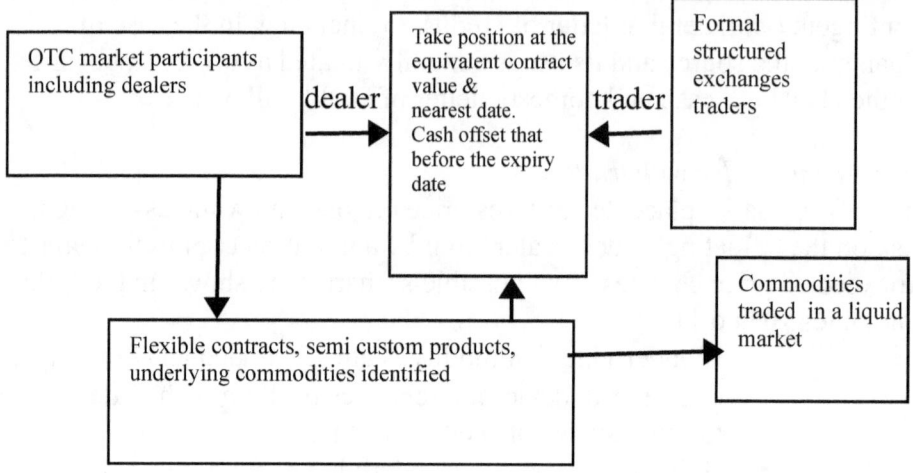

Fig. 7 : the present form of hedging in different trading platforms

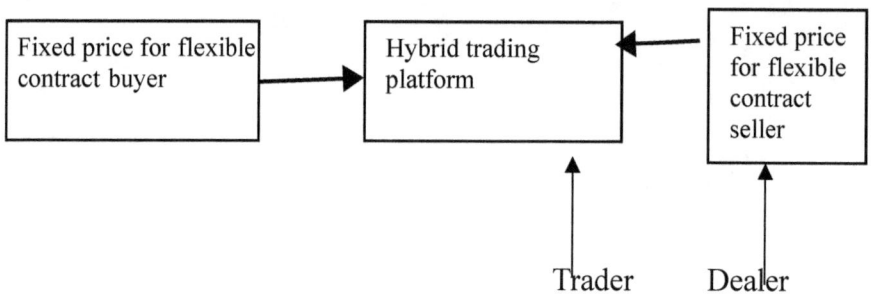

Fig. 8: HTP application in an OTCc marketplace

CHAPTER II
Pricing of derivatives

The following table compares different derivative[1] products in terms of flexibility and liquidity.

Comparison table

Derivatives	Contracts	Value/ price	Quantity	Delivery points	Settlement	Cost	Marketplace
Spot /cash	Bi-lateral	Fixed	Open	Mutually agreed	Physical	High	Unorganized
Futures	Standardized, Multi lateral	Float	Fixed	Fixed location	Cash offset/ physical	Low	Structured
Forwards/ swaps	Bi-lateral	Fixed, float	Any	Mutually agreed	Cash offset/ physical	High	OTC
Hybrid trading platform	Std cell, Multi-lateral	Limited float	Fixed small lot	Designated bonded warehouses	Cash offset/ physical	Low	Single platform

Table 1

An effective pricing of product requires liquidity and hence a competitive marketplace. Other requirements are full information related to trade which include price transparency and instantaneous dissemination. Here are the highlights.

- Volatility increases the risk premium and hence less efficient pricing. Certain types of derivatives add to volatility and therefore create more market instability.
- In forwards market, parties matter whereas in futures "perfect" substitution ensures fungibility.
- As hedgers become dominant participants, the risk premium increases, meaning futures' equilibrium prices get farther away from expected futures prices. This is shown in Fig. 1, below with explanation.

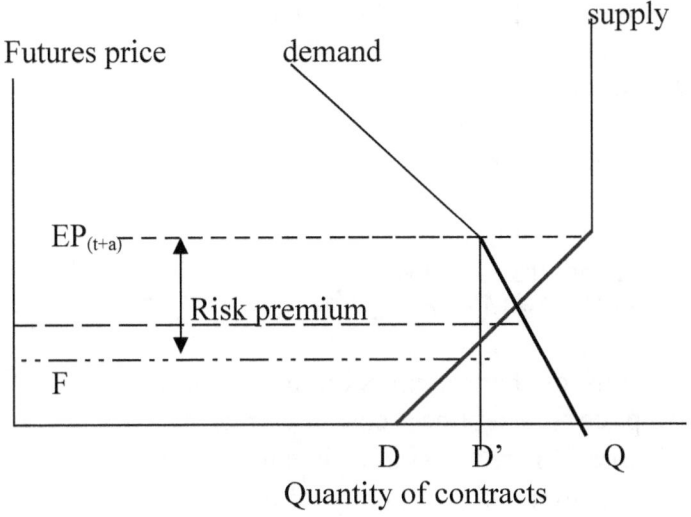

Fig 1: futures pricing explanation[2]

EP: expected price
F: equilibrium price
Q: all positions are hedged

In this example the market is all participants are hedgers; as such net short hedging represents bear market position.

Pricing of forwards

The following assumptions are made.

Futures(t,T)-cash(t)= basis(t,T)

If there is no arbitrage:

$1/(1+Rac) Tac = 1/(1+Rab)Tab * 1/(1+Rabc)Tbc$

raw data supplied

ac=06 months

T(ac)=6/12

ab=03 months

T(ab)=3/12

abac=bc=36 months

T(bc)=3/2 months= 45 days

$1/(1+r\ 06)6/12 = 1/(1+r\ 03)3/12*1/(1+r\ 36)3/2$

Definition and terms of above expressionsare as follows.

- forward price = cash price + cost of carry;
- cost of carry = interest cost-asset income;
- asset income for most commodity items=0.

Asset income for some assets such as currencies could be dividend or interest bearing asset income;for some assets incomes like equities and bonds, in the form of lump sum income.

F= Spot(1+interest per number of days/day count basis)

Example 1

Forward price, 30 days for cash market of $10,000 and annual interest rate of 12% is as follows.

- Day 1: 10,000(1+12*30/360/100)=10,000+100=10,100.
- Other factors: supply and demand and time decay.
- Day 2: F1=10,000(1+12*29/360/100)+ D; also a new 30 day forward is created.
- D= the delta of forward price on day one and forward price of Day 2.
- The new contract F2 = 9,850(1+12*30/360/100)= 9,850+98.5=9948.5.
- Day 3: F1=10,000(1+12*28/360/100)+D';
- D'= delta of 10,000 and forward price of day 3;
- F2=9,850 (1+12*29/360/100)+D".

The new contract F3=10,200(1+12*30/360/100)=10,200+102=10,302.

Skipping the days followed from the 3rd to 24th we will arrive at day 25, when contract F1 expires. Refer to Table 2, below.

Table 2: Forwards pricing

values of Forwards	Day 1	Day 2	Day 3	Day 4	Day 5	Days 6-24	DAY 25
Contract F1	10,100	10097-a	10093-b	10090+c	10087	na	expiration
Contract F2		9948	9945+b'	9942+c'		na	ditto
Contract F3			10302	10298		na	ditto

Pricing based on fixed calendar date

- Fix 36 periods for one year (10th and 20th and 30th)
- For every 30 day forward there will be 4 fixed sub-period of 7 days
- Assume 28 days for 30 day forward, etc.
- All contracts for 1-8 assume the standard 30th or 1st of month
- All contracts for 9-16 assume 20th day of the month
- All contracts for 17-25 assume 10th day of the month
- All contracts beyond 26th assume the position of new month.

Example 2
30-day delivery contract (red line)
60-day delivery contract (blue line)

Table 3: delivery expiration incrementally

Trading period	spot	June 10	June 20	June 30	July 10	July 20	July 30	Aug 20
May 26,29,30,31			▬			▬		
June 1-8				▬			▬	
June 9-16					▬			
June 17-26						▬		▬

Single platform for cash forwards and derivatives[3]

The risk of doing futures is inability to buy (or find) in cash market because spot market is too weak for now. This is in contrast to currency(or other established cash markets) where the volume of cash market is as big as forwards.

Table 4: cash forward trading: 30 day forward contract (contracts at 1000 lot)

Trading days	Forward price	Spot price	Delivery date	June 01	June 10	June 15	June 20 price
May 30	6.75	7.00	June 20	7.10			
May 31	7.45	8.00	June 20	7.10			
June 1	8.25	10.00	June 20		10.19		
June 2	9.05	12.00	June 20		10.19		
June 5	9.95	13.50	June 30		10.19		
June 6	10.95	16.00	June 30		10.19		
June 7	11.95	18.50	June 30		10.19		
June 8	11.00	17.00	June 30		10.19		
June 9	11.10	16.80	July 10			10.50	
June 12	12.00	18.00	July 10			10.50	
June 13	11.00	16.00	July 10			10.50	
June 14	10.00	14.50	July 10			10.50	
June 15	9.50	14.00	July 10			10.50	
June 16	9.36	14.10	July 10				9.84
June 19	10.00	14.20	July 20				9.84
June 20	10.25	14.00	July 20				9.84
June 21	9.85	13.50	July 20				9.84
June 22	9.75	13.00	July 20				9.84
June 23	9.85	14.00	July 20				9.84

Explanation:

Thirty day contract traded on May 30 was priced at $6.75. It expires on or about June 23. Thirty day contract traded on May 31 was priced at $7.45 marked-to-market price for margin maintenance on June1st for both contracts is $7.10 the average price of May 30 and May 31

The above contracts will have $10.19 as M-to-M from June 1st thru June 8th, $10.50 M-to-M from June 9 thru June 15 and $9.84 M-to-M for June 16 thru June 25 (expiry date)

Single platform for multiple marketplaces

Futures contract with HTP forwards in a single platform is demonstrated in Table 5 showing the complementary nature of existing industrial and financial commodities' futures with respect to forwards as the HTP's fulfillment.

Table 5: ALL CONTRACTS IN SINGLE PLATFORM

Complementary elements	Financial market	Industrial	The existing barrier	The HTP fulfillment
Risk	Interest rate	Underlying commodity	Open market not yet organized	Marketplace will attract participants and hence liquidity
Contract	Swap	Forwards	Contract /product	Methodology to develop contract/product
Price	Cost of capital	Cost of goods	Data transparency	Liquidity will lead to data transparency
Products	Bond futures complements swaps futures	Forwards and futures	Exchange	HTP methodlogy
Vision	Swap futures complement swap market	Forward futures complement forwards market	Forwards market	HTP single platform

37

Chapter III
Product design

A tradable product

Product offering is an important function of any marketplace. Generally, the tradability of a tangible products is most sectors such as mining, agricultural and industrial are selective and well advertised. Tradability, however, must satisfy the key criteria. A major criterion is the pre-existing liquid cash market; another requirement is unrestricted supply or demand. These pre-requisites constrain the implied liquidity of a product. For example, a large volume of trade requires almost unlimited availability of tradable products.

To identify tradable products, therefore, require an extensive market research to ascertain that the selected products would indeed be a "successful" product in terms of liquidity and trade volume. While there is no sure bet that a selected product is successful, there are nevertheless several issues that will have to be fully explored to ensure high level of confidence to propose a product for trade. They are formulated below.

The criteria for product selection, presently are tailored for structured exchange traded model, but they are fundamental enough to cover trading of most derivatives. They include size, volatility, source of public information (such as supply and demand), existence of dealer community and most important, the liquidity factor that is considered an instrument for risk management . We have selected a specific in-process-materials (IPM) for semiconductors to addresses the following pre-requisites.

- *Will the proposed marketplace operate on the basis of the available information?*

There is currently a good source of supply of public information with respect to supply and demand as well as price history for most of the proposed products. All manufacturing sectors are served by independent market research firms that routinely identify and provide the necessary data. In the United States such available information can be verified by data gathered from the US Government agencies.

- *Can the proposed contracts be sold to corporate buyers and sellers as an improved mechanism for risk management?*

The existing marketplace for primary metals and energy serves an older, more mature generation of manufacturing sectors. Most manufacturers experience the classic forward contracts with its inherent drawback when price at delivery date becomes an issue. It may be concluded that minimizing the cost of storage and or inventory, as well as the concept of price discovery would provide strong and logical- economic justifications for shifting risks from tangible assets to paper trade.

- *How can the question of liquidity be resolved?*

Electronic trading environment allows manufacturers to constantly monitor the best bid and offer. The best bid and offer, in turn, are generated from such inquiries resulted from order placing. We expect that only 8% to15% of all inquiries from manufacturers lead to orders and that will be 80% of total transactions at a given period. This is in contrast to floor trading with 40% to 60% percent of orders being generated by a limited number of floor brokers. As discussed in chapter I, various methods are employed to encourage liquidity such as allowing an open and easy participation of electronic traders and manufacturers (as bid and offers)thereby creating a marketplace with credible depth which in turn would lead to a realistic spread range for a given product.

- *Is there sufficient volatility ?*

Every product introduced will be chosen on the basis of certain known historical data. The price history with its fluctuation is obviously an important one. The selected product is expected to be responsive to primary source of raw material, market demand and global economic conditions. Not every product is, of course, volatile at all times

- *And the size with respect to market efficiency?*

The most important element of change from floor to electronic trading occurs in market cost efficiency and transaction frequency. A product may only be traded fifty times a day, but because it is traded electronically it is still cost efficient when compared to floor- which requires a large multiple of that to become cost effective. The size of daily contracts, depending on the products, could be as low as hundreds. The cost efficiency is still maintained because of non existing costs associated with floor trading.

- *Is there an existing broker community ?*

The manufacturing sectors follow various channels of distribution, but in each sector there are brokers that take titles of the goods and resell them. These resellers and or brokers may not take physical possession of the goods for any period depending on the market condition. In some industries such as chemical the brokering business has replaced the classical distribution channel in most places. Brokers simply take over titles and resell them. In electronics business, large quantities of chips are brokered routinely and globally in a secondary market. All these brokers operate within a fractured and dysfunctional community.

Product Design Process
Once the fundamental questions about the marketing of industry's or sector's products are addressed we can proceed with the general construction of "cell" or root products. First an industry followed by a sector must be selected. A "tree" is then constructed representing major product groups of that sector. Each group is further analyzed to search for the root product. To avoid unnecessary and cumbersome job of listing all and every product through-out the process we adopt the principal of 80/20 rule. An interpretation of Pareto's (Distribution) Law is explained below.

The 80/20 Rule Simplified
Generally, the rule states that 80 percent of any subject category constitutes 20 percent of the particular property related to the subject. For example, within a defined demography 20 percent manufacturers, in a given industry, may well control 80% of the market in that sector. The rule is valid for any applications. As an application of this rule about 20 percent of materials used in a given manufacturing process contribute to about 80 percent of the   material cost . Conversely, we can assume that 20 percent of all manufacturers goods in, say, electronics industry dominate 80 percent of the electronics business.

Example
A Methodology for applying the 80/20 rule to the Bill of Materials (BOM) used in batch manufacturing is outlined below. The approach is generally valid and is not limited to manufacturer's bill of materials. See figure 2.

- List all items required for batch production.
- Exclude all MOR (materials for operation and repair).
- Calculate total inventory, both at hand and to-be purchased.
- Calculate 80% of the Dollar amount of above.

- Sort on the order of highest value, i.e quantity times purchased price.
- Add items descending until the total approaches or equals the figure of 80%
- Calculate the number of items that has produced the above figure.
- If total of selected items is greater than 20% of total numbers add 20% of items downward.
- Calculate subtotal value.
- If total is less than 80% of total add items downward until total approaches 80%
- Repeat steps 8-10 until 20% is reached within approximation.

Information gathering

The idea of collecting information is most time sensitive. In today's wired world the timeliness of information is more important of the content detail, or full accuracy. The bulk of market intelligence can be extracted and updated from news original sources that are routinely published. This section attempts to describe a structural design for a database from which the critical data can be retrieved. Initially the database requires that the collected text or data be edited and inputted. Relatively sophisticated search engine will then allow the researcher to retrieve the requested data. In this chapter we will touch upon certain aspects of taxonomy which will be employed to improve the quality of text/data collection on the Internet by an agent.

The main categories of news and information database, for a given sector, are outlined below.
- Marketplace (spot market, broker, others)
- Products (technology, currency, availability)
- Company , suppliers and consumers (financial & operational)
- Cottage industry (engineering service, market research, sales)

A Taxonomy detailing a logical hierarchical classification of sector and relationships among all the categories, will reduce complexity of data collection. It supplements text retrieval and results in higher quality of information. The process contains the following steps.

- Creation
- Updating

41

- Dissemination
- Consumption

Generally, life cycle of a document(text and data) extends from creation, reviewing, distribution, updating to archiving and deletion.

The following schema shows a comparison of taxonomy application of text retrieval with standard data mining. The difference is the quality of text or in summary a structured versus unstructured data type. It remains to know the content residency and how it should be shared.

	Data mining	Filter (DB)	
Automatic →	Text mining	text retrieval	
			SQL
Manual →	total analysis system Tool for populating	text retrieval spreadsheet	
	Discrete Look at everything	Sift Look at small point	

The core team is needed to decide what content and how to retrieve. The sequence of events are listed below.

- Creating content, items (identify, inventory and analyze) using analysis engine.
- Creating (starter), trial population and refinement.
- Publishing.
- Maintenance.

As an example, let us consider the manufacturing sector which is, generally, defined based on the marketplace, the nature of manufacturing, its products and the supporting industries.

Manufacturing sector

marketplaces
- market fundamentals
- statistics
- market data ◀———————————
- market sentiments
- inter-markets
- producers/consumers

Operation
- plants & equipment
- production capacity
- people on the move
- new products
- new plants

financial
- Financial statement
- Investment
- Merger and acquisition

Analysis
- sales data
- operating margin
- market data digest ◀————————

Product
- Shelf life status
- Technology
- Market share

Supporting industry
- Sales (trade show, seminar,..)
- Engineering support
- Government liaison and PR
- Trade association
- Trade publication

Now that the methodology for data retrieval is established we can proceed with design of tables to construct the required database. Database construction consists of tables that generally contain the following.

Manufacturers' information stored in database
- Company, identification, product 1, product 2, product 3;
- Product, description, identification, industry market share
- Identified product, spot closing in major currencies, 30-day moving average, later, forwards(average closing)
- Sales contribution, sales, Earnings Before Tax, regional sales

Industry knowledge
- Compute market shares of products individually and collectively
- Identifying industry leadership in manufacturing
- Compiling list of industry's major players
- Understanding how manufacturing classification (such as SIC) is organized example
- Selecting a manufacturing sector(see table below)

Selecting manufacturing segments

Industry	public co's	private co's	Total sale	top 1000	SIC
Computer	208	1150	140b	29	3571
Electronics	252	1200	30	14	3672/79
Chemical & plastics	105	1100	115	42	2812/99
Pharmaceutical	156	800	125	27	2831/65
Refinery products	28	390	320	18	2911
Pulp & paper	51	950	62	32	2611/76
Tire & rubber	6	600	21	13	3011/69
Ferrous metals	49	920	23	17	3312/35
Non ferrous met.	36	1150	36	11	3334/57
Electrical	56	750	130	10*	3612/48
Glass	10	200*	13	2	1793
Textile	48	400	20	8	2235/59
Transport equipment	11	200*	5	2	3799/5088
Total	1016	9810	1046	225	------

The relative importance of these manufacturing sectors is determined by statistical data.

Intermediate Goods	% relative importance
Commercial electrical power	4.197
Industrial chemical	4.05
Motor vehicle parts	3.780
Industrial electrical power	3.249
Steel mill products	3.198
Fabricated structured metal products	2.899
Electronics components	2.668
Misc metal products	2.244
Plastic, resins	2.002
paper board	1.260
Paper boxed and containers	2.165
paper	2.077
Finished fabrics	1.137
Jet fuel	0.926
Prepared print	0.878
Number two diesel fuel	0.840
Processed yarn & thread	0.734

Compiling industry's major products for sectors is shown below.

Industry	Number of public companies	Market size/ annual sale	Sector targeted	Average growth rate
electronics	800	$100 billion	Semi conductor	11%
chemical	300	$ 90 billion	plastics	4%
automotive	20	Billions, annual/na	Auto parts	9%, estimated

The next step is then to analyze the sales and marketing of each company.

electronic companies	*projected sales	Global market share	Commodity index1	Commodity index2	Contribution to sales/cost of goods	Currency translation[1]
micron	16.4 billion	14.4%,1999	memories	NA	73%	2 billion
Compaq/H-P	111 billion	< 10%, 2004	printers	pc	52%	10 billion

* last quarter, 2014; NA- not available

Some data may be found from the following sources;
- compiling shipped products requires personal relationship;
- agent is needed to collect prices from e-commerce sources

Market intelligence research

Once the key products are identified, the general criteria for researching a product need the following market knowledge about the particular product.

- Market size (Total Available Market)
- Market data availability (or accessibility). This feature implies the existence of an open market allows the price and supplied quantities would be easily accessible.
- Product's cash market size is a pre-requisite for selecting the product; it ensures the potential for its forward price liquidity and viabilty.
- Multi-currency trade; each product is traded in a market's local currency. This implies that the normal daily fluctuation of the marketplace's currency will be added to the already existing market fluctuation of the product.
- Product technical specification and life cycle.

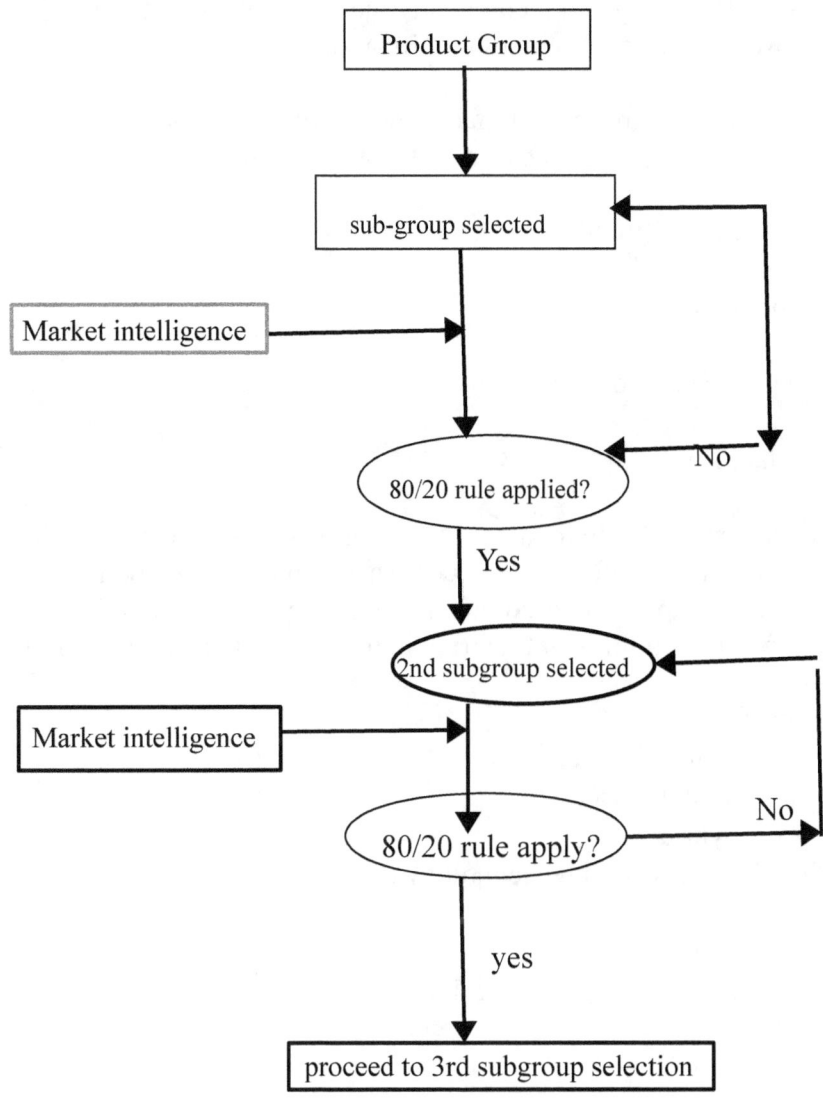

Fig. 2- Product selection based on 80/20 rule

The rationale for product selection is based on the criterion that the product is non proprietary and theoretically inexhaustible. A fungible product follows a universal standard specification.

Electronics, the single largest manufacturing sector, is our chosen industry. The selected products based on the above criteria are

- Integrated Circuits

- Interconnects

- Passive components

- Chemicals

Each group is further sub-divided until the final products are derived. The end product must satisfy all the above criteria and must be a market share leader within its group. Market dominance of particular subdivided products shown in bold follow 80/20 rule in the Integrated Circuit market.

IC market:
- analog devices
- digital devices
- hybrids
digital devices employ technology of:
- cmos
- bipolar
digital devices using cmos technology:
- standard cell
- ASIC
- memories
- logic devices

Next, the taxonomy principle may be applied to construct a database for every selected product.

Identification data
- Manufacturer Part number decoder
- prefix identifying, manufacturer, trade mark, others
- suffix identifying specification for a particular part
- product classification identifying product group
- identified root product

Technical data
- physical characteristic
- electrical properties
- environmental
- material

Engineering
- design feature
- packaging/enclosure
- organization

Standards
- form factor
- code

Technology
- die
- process

Examples of value-added stages
Manufactured value-added products begin from primary stage of production(for example, crude oil extraction), secondary(adding chemical to make refined gasoline) followed by further stage of reformulating)and so on.

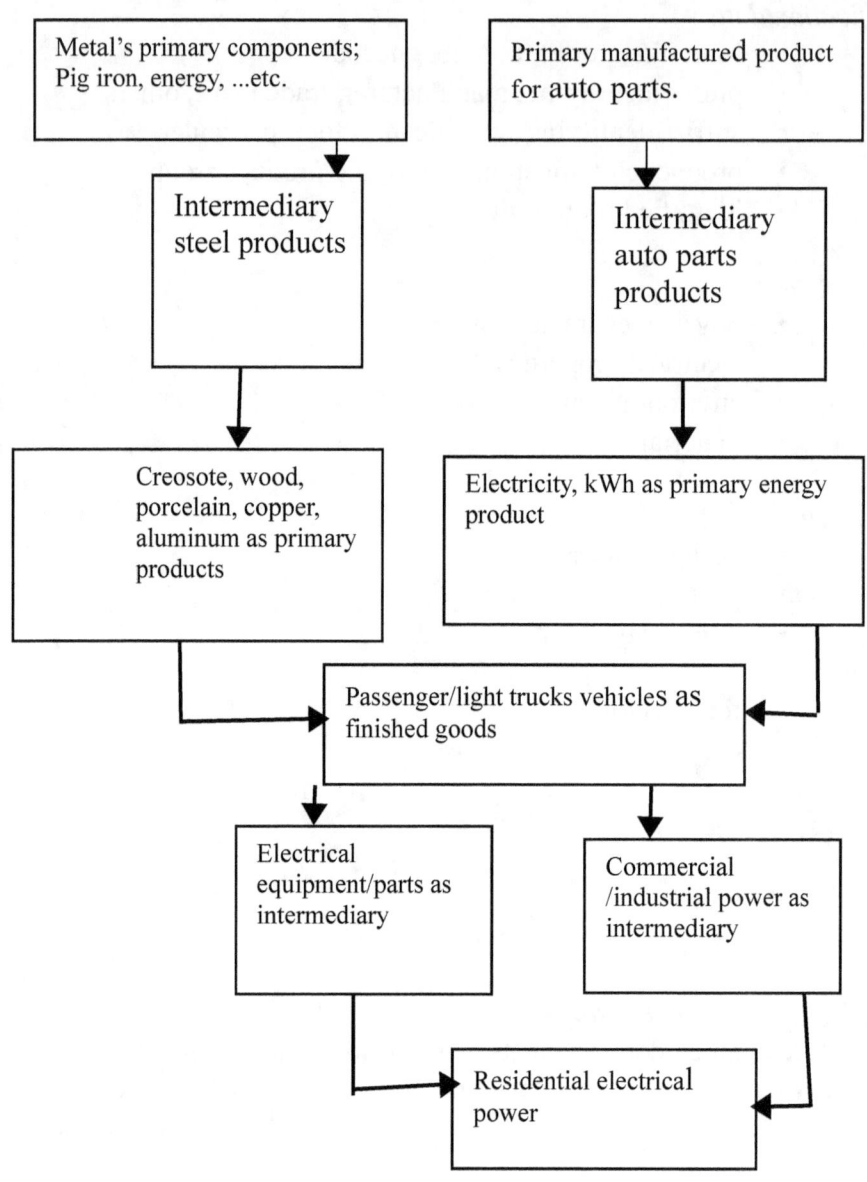

Fig. 3: Selection of industry process

INDEXING

Index represents composite value of a group of items. Generally an index devisor is the sum of items divided by 100. Calculate *devisor* and follow the steps for price indexing.

- Group products that are all in the same class;

- list previous prices of related products;

- calculate the delta and multiply that columns which contains "product id" and related products 1, 2,3,4...

- repeat for each column containing product id, product price change, related product price, ...etc.

The following columns contain product id, related group product prices 1,2,3,... formula.

Commodity traded	Current closing price of traded commodity	Previous closing price of traded commodity	Targeted Commodity last price	New targeted commodity price
P:1Mx16 MB,EDO, 50 ns, DIP	$4.25	$4.35	$4.65	$4.6
As above	$4.25	$4.00	$4.65	$4.81
As above	$4.25	$4.75	$5.00	$4.75
As above	$4.25	$5.00	$5.00	$4.625

- Product P average closing price for period $T_1 = Z_{t1}$
- Product P previous average closing price for period $T_2 = Z_{t2}$
- Delta $(Z_{t2} - Z_{t1}) = [w]$
- Product P_1 last price for period $X = Z_1$
- Product P_1 adjusted price for period $X = Z_1 + Z_{1[w]}$

[ ] indicates absolute value.

Index calculation

In concept, the Producer Price Index is calculated according to a modified Laspeyres formula, where:

P_o is the price of a commodity in the comparison period;
P_i is its price currently; and
Q_a represents the quantity shipped during the weight-base period.

An alternative formula approximates the actual computation procedure more closely. In this form, the index is the weighted average of price relatives, i.e., price ratios for each item (P_i /P_o). The expression ($Q_a P_o$) represents the weights in value form. The elements P and Q originally relate to period "a" but are adjusted for price change to period "0"and are not derived separately. When specifications or samples change, the item's relatives must be then computed by linking i.e., multiplying the relatives for respective periods for which the data are precisely comparable.

References

Information currently used for calculating weights throughout the PPI family of indexes is largely taken from the following censuses conducted

by the Bureau of the Census of the U.S. Department of Commerce:

(i) *Census of Manufactures;*

(ii) *Census of Mineral Industries* which includes oil and gas production;

(iii) *Census of Agriculture;* and

(iv) *Census of Service Industries.*

Other current weight sources include the Energy Information Administration of the U.S. Department of Energy and the National Marine Fisheries Service of the U.S. Department of Commerce.

A general description of how seasonal adjustment procedures are typically applied at BLS is given in appendix A at the end of the Handbook.

See "On the Use of Intervention Analysis in Seasonal Adjustment" by J. A. Buszuwski and S. Scott, Proceedings of the Business and Economics Section, American Statistical Association, 1988.

Summary of procedure to calculate indexes
The first step is to specify a product group. Then the following steps are required.

- Determine the entire breakdown.
- Research total available market for each subgroup, sub-subgroup, etc in dollars.
- Determine TAM for traded product items in dollars.
- Determine closing spot prices for each item.
- If TAM is not available calculate that by multiplying shipped quantity and spot price.
- Calculate the change in index for a given period (delta * previous index).
- Use simple average for calculating each sub-subgroup, subgroup and group index example of calculating index;
  - list all similar items within the cell index
  - gather closing spot prices for each item at a given time
  - gather aggregated shipment for above date
  - calculate sum of shipment times spot closing
  - divide sum for aggregate shipment to obtain average price
  - divide sum by T1 - T0 and multiply by 100 to obtain Index.

Example

Table A: Products' identification for constructing index

Products traded in group	Market share (sub-subgroup)	TAM, US	Market share (subgroup)	TAM, global	Market share (group)
4Mx16 SDRAM	65%	14,000,000,000	70%	20,000,000,000	70%
4M flash	0%	1,500,000,000	50%	3,000,000,000	10%
128k SRAM	40%	960,000,000	80%	3,000,000,000	10%

Table B: Continuation of Table A

Product Traded	Description	Cell index	Sub-subgroup index	Sub-group index	group index
SDRAM	Memory	4x16 64m: 62.3 16m: 43.33 128m:73.16	SDRAM: 66.68 EDO: 50.86 FPM: 47.05	SDRAM: 62.20 SRAM: 45.90 FLASH: 44.66	All Memories 59.13
0805 X7R	Ceramic cap				

Table C: Continuation, sub-subgroup level for index construction

Targeted commodity	Commodity traded	Current closing price	Previous closing price	Targeted Commodity last price	New targeted comm. price
P1:1Mx16 MB,EDO, 50ns, SOP	P:1Mx16 MB, EDO, 50ns, DIP	$4.25	$4.35	$4.65	4.6
P2: 4Mx4 EDO, 50ns, DIP	As above	$4.25	$4.00	$4.65	4.81
P3: 1mx16 SDRAM, DIP	As above	$4.25	$4.75	$5.00	4.75
P4. 16mx1, FPM, 60ns, DIP	As above	$4.25	$5.00	$5.00	4.625

Index Calculation: $4.65- ($4.35-$4.25)* $4.65=$4.60…

Contract Design

The main characteristics of contracts, as tabulated in Figure 14, are product dependent. The system is based on semi-custom product design which means for each specific end product the contract has to be specifically stated.

- hybrid forward
- cash market
- single platform
- multi-currency (Euro &Yen)
- small lot size
- tick value (minimum fluctuation)

As product is specified, the system will update or adjust the contract property for lot size, product specification and tick value. It also adjusts the daily limit and performance bond required for the contract. The system is also adjusts hours of trading and the currency of trade based on selected marketplace. Contract design essentials are tabulated below.

Product	Name (any) Description (any) Unit (no, pounds, ton, gallon, ounce) Lot size (10,100,1000,10000,20000, 50000) Code (any)
Delivery	Date (30, 60, 90, every 15 day)notice dates (T-x1, T-x2)
Trading	Marketplace (hybrid, futures, spot), all months hours (8am-2pm EST), (9am-3pm PST), (11am-5pm GMT), (9am-3pm Pacific); week begins (Sunday, Monday). Week ends (Friday 5 pm PST)
Pricing	Minimum fluctuation (1/100. 1/20, 1/10 of currency). Daily limit (percentage of nominal contract value; 5%, 6%,7%,8%,9%,10%). Currency (usd & euro, usd & jpy, usd & local currency). Strike price is not available
Clearing	Electronic: • single source interfacing • multi source interfacing
Settlement	• Cash offset • Physical delivery
Liquidity	• Virtual market maker • Open book for matching

Table D: Contract specification

APPENDIX I

Example of product classification

group 1: memories

subgroup 1-1: dram

sub-subgroup 1-1-1: CMOS hi performance, fast page mode,5v,1mx1, 60ns

sub-sub-subgroup   1-1-1-1-1 : 18 pin, dip; and

           1-1-1-1-2 : 26/20 pin, soj

sub-subgroup 1-1-2 : CMOS hi performance, fast page mode,5v,4mx1,60ns

sub-sub-subgroup   1-1-2-1-1: 18 pin, dip; and

           1-1-2-1-1 :26/20 pin, soj

sub-subgroup 1-1-3 : CMOS hi performance, fast page mode,5v, 4mx4, 60ns,4k refresh

sub-sub-subgroup 1-1-3-1:28/24 pin, soj

group 1: memory devices

subgroup 1-2 : sram

sub-subgroup 1-2-1BiCMOS hi speed static RAM

organized as 128kx8, plastic dip, 5 v, async, 32 pin

sub-sub-subgroup   1-2-1-1-1:   20 ns; and

           1-2-1-1-2 :   15 ns

sub-subgroup 1-2-2   : standard static RAM, organized as 32kx8, 3-5 v, 28 pin

sub-sub-subgroup   1-2-2-1-1: 85 ns; and

           1-2-2-1-2 :100 ns.

subgroup 1-2-2 : CMOS hi speed static RAM

organized as 32kx8, plastic dip, 5 v,async, 28 pin

sub-sub-subgroup   1-2-2-1 : 35 ns;and

           1-2-2-2 :20 ns.

group 2 : IC,

subgroup 2-1 : logic devices

sub-subgroup 2-1-1 : cmos 74hc series, -55 to 125 c, with soic packaging

sub-sub-subgroups	2-1-1-1-1 :	and gates(quad 2-input);
	2-1-1-1-2	nand gates(quad 2-input);
	2-1-1-1-3	nor gates (ditto);
	2-1-1-1-4	buffers (hex inverter);
	2-1-1-1-5	latches (octal transparent, 3-state, non inverting);
	2-1-1-1-6	flip-flop(octal d, 3 state).

group 3: *passive devices*
subgroup3-1 : capacitors
sub-subgroup3-1-1: ceramic
sub-sub-subgroup 3-1-1-1: smd, multi-layer, g.p.,X7R form factor, 50V, 4700pf
sub-sub-sub-subgroup   3-1-1-1-1   1206;
                                       3-1-1-1-2   0805;
                                         3-1-1-1-3   0603;
                                         3-1-1-1-4   0402.

group 3 : passive devices
subgroup 3-1: capacitors
sub-subgroup 3-1-1': film
sub-sub-subgroup   3-1-1'-1: metalized polystyrene epoxy, g.p[2], 4700pf+-2%
sub-sub-sub-subgroup   3-1-1-1'-1   50wv
                                         3-1-1-1'-2   100wv
                                         3-1-1-1'-3   250wv

group 3: passive devices
subgroup 3-2: resistors
sub-subgroup   3-2-1: thick film chip resistor[3].
sub-sub-subgroup   3-2-1-1-1   0603
                                         3-2-1-1-2   1206
                                         3-2-1-1-3   0803
sub-sub-subgroup   3-2-2-1: thick film resistor network[4]

Group 4-: connector
subgroup 4-1 : IC socket
sub-subgroup 4-1-1 : PLCC, .050" outer spacing, smt
sub-sub-subgroup   4-1-1-1   44 circuit
                                         4-1-1-2   68 circuit
                                         4-1-1-3   84 circuit
group 4: connector
subgroup 4-1 : IC socket
sub-subgroup 4-1-2 : PGA (pin grid array), .050" ZIF
sub-sub-subgroup   4-1-2-1   68 pin
                                         4-1-2-2   84 pin
                                         4-1-2-3   132 pin

group 4: connector
subgroup 4-2 : SIMM socket
sub-subgroup　　4-2-1: dual row, metal latch, vertical, SIMM socket, .050"
sub-sub-subgroup　　4-2-1-1　　　0.050x0.300"
　　　　　　　　　　4-2-1-2　　　0.100x0.300"

group 4: connector
subgroup 4-3 : IDC
sub-subgroup:　　　4-3-1: double sided, .100", 10-64 position
sub-sub-subgroup : 4-3-1-1　　edge header
　　　　　　　　　　4-3-1-2　　box
　　　　　　　　　　4-3-1-3　　socket
group 4: connector
subgroup 4-4 : D-sub (cable)
sub-subgroup: 4-4-1: D-sub, metal shell with mounting holes
sub-sub-subgroup　　4-4-1-1　　　9 pin male or female
　　　　　　　　　　4-4-1-2　　　37 pin male
　　　　　　　　　　4-4-1-3　　　37 pin female

APPENDIX II

Example of index calculation from a group(memory) to subgroup(types), to sub-subgroup(capacity) and sub-sub-subgroup(organization); not necessarily in that order.

SUB-SUB-SUBGROUP: 128MB(megabit) capacity

market size distribution

0.1   0.81b   0.4b   0.2b

32mx4   16mx8   8mx16   others(pc133, ddr,rd)
12-4-00 closing spot	$8.00	$6.85	$7.20
shipped before previous change	25000	10000	7500
12-19-00 closing spot	$7.75	$6.75	$7.00
shipped this period	18000	7500	6000

Average price for 128m: $7.375
Average previous price: $7.589
Index of 128m is as follows.

100(18000*7.75+7500*6.75+6000*7(25000*8+10000*6.85+7500*7.2)=73.18

SUB-SUBGROUP BREAKDOWN OF 64 MB

market size distribution not available

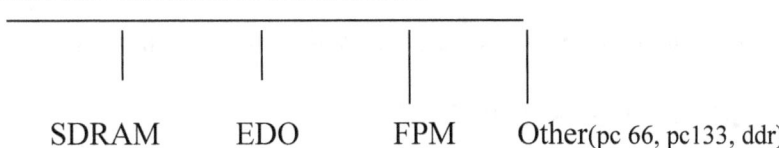

SDRAM   EDO   FPM   Other(pc 66, pc133, ddr)

SUB-SUB-SUBGROUP: 64 MB SDRAM (cell index)

market size distribution:

2.5b	1.5 b	1b
4MBx16	16MBx4	8MBx8

Other(pc 66, pc133, ddr):

	4MBx16	16MBx4	8MBx8
shipped in previous period	75,000	30,000	20,000
shipped in this period	55,000	20,000	10,000
closing spot as of 12-4-00	$4.00	$3.75	$4.25
currently as of 12-19-00	$3.50	$3.75	$4.25

I=100(55000*3.5+20000*3.75+10000*4.25/75000*4+30000*3.75+20000*4.25)=62
Average price (for 64 M): $4.05
Average previous price: $3.98

SUB-SUB-SUBGROUP: 64 MB EDO

market size distribution not available

	4mx16	8mx8	16mx4	other
closing spot on 12-04-00	$5.25	$12.00	$16.50	na
shipped previous..	25,000	7000	6000	na
closing spot on 12-19-00	$4.75	$11.50	$14.75	na
shipped this period	15,000	5000	4000	na
Average price for 64 EDO on 12-04-00	$ 8.27			
Average price on 12-19-00	$ 7.80			

I:100(15000*4.75+5000*11.5+4000*14.75(25000*5.25+7000*12+6000*16.5)=59.74

SUB-SUB-SUBGROUP: 64MB FPM

market size distribution not available

	4mx16	8mx8	16mx4	other
closing spot on 12-04-00:	$4.95?	$13.50	12.5	na
shipped	15,000	7000	5500	na
closing spot on 12-19-00	$4 .00	$13.00	$12	na
shipped	10,000	5000	2000	na

60

Average price on 12-04-00 $8.64
Average price on 12-19-00 $7.58

I=100(10000*4+5000*13+2000*12(15000*4.95+7000*13.5+5500*12.5)=54.31

SUB-SUBGROUP 16MB(megabit): NO DATA

market size distribution not available

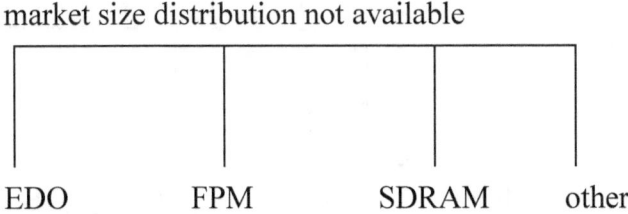

EDO	FPM	SDRAM	other

SUB-SUB-SUBGROUP: 16MB EDO

Index for 16 m EDO

	market size distribution:		
	0.5b	0.2b	0.3b
	1mx16	4mx4	others
previous closing spot:	$3.75	$4.55	$3.5
shipped	25,000	12,000	15,000
12-19-00 spot	$3.75	$4.00	$3.5
shipped in this period	18,000	8,000	10,000
Average price for 16M:	$3.74		
Previous average price:	$3.86		

I=100(18000*3.75+8000*4+10000*3.5/25000*3.75+12000*4.55+15000*3.5)=66.98

SUB-SUB-SUBGROUP: 16M FPM

market size distribution not available

	1mx16	16mx1	4mx4	other
closing spot 12-04-00	$4.75	3.75	5.50	
shipped	30,000	15000	12000	na
closing spot 12-19-00	$4.75	$3.25	$4.50	na
shipped	18000	7500	8000	na

61

Average price on 12-04-00 $4.65
Average price on 12-19-00 $4.35

I:100(18000*4.75+7500*3.25+8000*4.5/(30000*4.75+15000*3.75+12000*5.5)=55.10

SUB-SUB-SUBGROUP: 16MB SDRAM

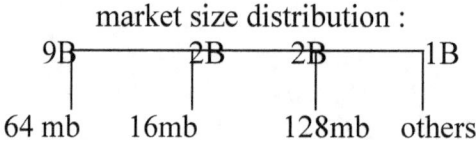

	market size distribution not available		
	1mx16	2mx8	Other
spot closing on 12-04-00	$3.75	$4.50	na
shipped	20000	na	na
spot closing 12-19-00	*3.25*	na	na
shipped	10000	na	na

No average pricing recorded
I =100(10000*3.25)/(20000*3.75)=43.33

Calculating index based on technology

SUB-SUBGROUP: SDRAM

market size distribution :

9B   2B   2B   1B

64 mb   16mb   128mb   others

SDRAM, PC-100 :

According to above breakdown simple average prices=5.12

Shipped according to above breakdown 187,500

12-19-00 closing spot: $5.06

shipped now: 85,000+36,000+32,000=153,000

according to above breakdown 126,500

Index of SDRAM= 100(153,000*5.055/219,000*5.143);accordingly

I=100(126500*5.06/187500*5.12)=66.68

SUB-SUBGROUP: EDO

	64m	16m	total
12-04-00	$10.56	$3.86	
total shipment	47000	52000	89000
12-19-00	$ 9.56	$3.74	
total shipment	23000	36000	59000

No average pricing recorded

I=100(23000*9.56+36000*3.75)/(47000*10.56+52000*3.86)
=100(354520)/(697040)=50.86

SUB-SUBGROUP: FPM

12-04-00	$7.13	$4.96	
shipment	27500	57000	84500
12-19-00	$6.58	$4.58	
shipment	17000	33500	50500

No average pricing recorded

I=100(17000*6.58+33500*4.58)/(27500*7.13+57000*4.96)=100(265290)/
(478795)==55.41

SUB-GROUP:DRAM

	1.4B SDRAM	2B EDO	2B FPM	1B DDR	1/2B RDR	1/2B other
12-04-00	$5.12	$7.21	$6.05	na	na	na
Shipment	187500	89000	84500			
12-19-00	$5.06	$6.65	$5.58	na	na	na
Shipment	126500	59000	50500			

No average prices recorded

I=100 (5.06*126500+6.65*59000+5.58*50500)/(5.12*187500+7.21*89000+6.05*84500)
I =100(1314230/ 2112915)=62.20

Closing spot price on 12-04-00	$5.85
Shipped then	361000
Shipped last	236000
Closing spot price on 12-19-00	$5.57

Computing SRAM, flash and other memories

SRAM:

estimated data on market size

0.5 b	0.2b	0.4b	0.1b	0.25b	0.1b
512x8 dip	512kx8tsop[5]	128kx8dip	128kx8sop	32kx8 fast cache	32kx8, slow

Average price on 12-04-00

| $10.00 | $9.50 | $5.50 | $4.50 | $1.85 | $2.35 | | |

Shipment

| 10000 | 3000 | 5000 | 0 | 4000 | na | na |

Average price on 12-19-00

| $10.00 | $9.50 | $5.50 | $4.50 | $1.85 | na | na |

Shipment

| 5000 | 1000 | 2000 | 1000 | 1500 | na | na |

$I=100(5000*10+1000*9.5+2000*5.5+1000*4.5)/$
$(10000*10+3000*9.5+5000*5.5+0+4000*1.85) =100(75000)/(163400)=45.90$

Average closing spot   12-04-00: $7.43
Average spot closing   12-19-00: $7.14

FLASH:

Data on market size distribution not available

32M	16M	8M	4M	1M

Closing spot on 12-04-00

| $30 | $15 | $11 | $7.00 | $5.0 |

Shipment

| 2000 | 5000 | 8000 | 10000 | 4000 |

Closing spot on 12-19-00

| $24 | $12.00 | $9.00 | $6.50 | $4.85 |

Shipment

| 1000 | 3000 | 4000 | 4500 | 3000 |

I=100(1000*24+3000*12+4000*9+4500*6.5+3000*4.85)/
(2000*30+5000*15+8000*11+10000*7+4000*5)=100(139800(313000)=44.66

Average spot 12-04-00:	$10.72
Shipment:	29000
Average spot closing 12-19-00:	$9.02
Shipment:	15500

MEMORY GROUP

	20B	3B	3B	1.5B	2.5B
	DRAM	RAM	FLASH	PROM	VRAM/GRAM
Closing spot 12-04-00	$5.85	$7.43	$10.72	na	na
Shipment	361000	22000	29000		
Closing spot 12-19-00	$5.57	$7.14	$9.02		
Shipment	23600	10500	15500		

I=100(236000*5.57+10500*7.14+15500*9.02) [divided by]:
(361000*5.85+22000*7.43+29000*10.72)
=100(1529300)/(2586190)=59.13

APPENDIX III
Contract specification for electronics group

PRODUCT	Semiconductors	Passive components	Connectors
Market	Pacific/US	US/ China	US/ Taiwan
Exchange	HTP	HTP	HTP
Trading hours	14hrs	12 hrs	12 hrs
Contract Size	500 units	10000 units	1000 units
Months traded all	months	tri- monthly	tri-monthly
Price quoted in		ALL CURRENCIES	
Minimum fluctuation	.05	.005	.01
Value of min. fluctuation	$25	$50	$10
Value 100 basis point	$500	$1000	$1000
Daily limit	TBD	none	none
Spot contract limit	none	none	none
First notice day	3rd Monday	3rd Monday	3rd Tuesday
Last trading day	last Friday	last Wednesday	last Thursday

Chapter IV
Straight through processing (STP)

Introduction

Straight through processing (STP) in securities industry is an end to end automation of the trading process between both buy and sell side institutions, on a single platform; it begins from the first capture of an order through to final settlement; it means a seamless, electronic transfer of information to all parties involved in the trading cycle utilizing standardized information flows, technologies and infrastructures.

From a customer's viewpoint the ability to achieve a fully integrated STP capability allows greater access to liquidity with a service linking all areas of the investment chain-brokers, institutions, exchanges, as well as private investors. In addition STP reduces errors such as input orders, speeding settlement, reducing risk and cost of capital.

Trends And Requirement For STP

Explosive growth of transaction levels in the securities market, particularly cross-border is fueled by privatization and personal pension provision for an aging population. Further more, online trading in the retail sector, boosted by private investors, with extended trading hours and new regulatory guidelines such as introduction of next day trade settlement, T+1, have added an urgency to seamless trading platform.

Volume growth

According to International Federation of Stock Exchanges Annual Report 1998, the total market capitalization for securities listed on the world's leading exchanges has grown to more than US $25,500 billion in 1998 and saw the volume of annual securities transactions worldwide jump from nearly 690 million in 1997 to nearly 835 million in 1998.

Cross-border transaction volumes, Global Straight Through Processing Association (GSTPA) claims, have increased exponentially and are forecast to be at around 600,000 securities transactions per day by 2002 versus 1998 - 200,000 per day. By November 2015 these numbers have increased significantly. For example, S & P 500 daily transactions' volume is more than millions shares.

Accomplishment of STP is complex. The institutions require price information, order capture, execution, links to settlement, clearing and custody all to be handled electronically. Sourcing the appropriate systems and their integration can be a major inhibitor.

The practical implementation of STP involves a number of processes: order processing which covers from inquiry to order routing;

- order execution, matching and order confirmation;
- connecting the front, middle and back offices;
- linkage to financial clearing and cash settlement;
- custody and safekeeping of physicals for non-cash settlement;
- participants connectivity at every stage .

The cost advantages of *STP*

The lack of straight through processing to handle the increasing volume of securities trades, according to S.W.I.F.T. as quoted in Straight Through Processing's A Forum for Change, Issue 1., 1999, is estimated to cost the securities' industry US $12 billion per annum. The current cost of correcting errors to maintain securities transactions accuracy is broken down as follows.

- 60% of settlement instructions require repair at a cost of US$ 6.00 per repair.
- 10% of confirms and statements result in mismatches at a cost of US$ 16.00 each.
- 15% of transactions fail to settle on time at a cost of US $50.00+ to resolve each failure.

The cash management module

The business models used in most trading businesses are of two types. The first is an operational process by which products and funds are transferred; they include calculation of parties obligations, collateral management and physical delivery. The second method involves the central counter-party, as settlement agent to all transactions conducted in the market. Settlement, in general, refers to exchange of money for goods as physical or paper, for which a contract may have been consummated. Cash settlement simply is a replacement for goods. It is a specified cash. The brokerage firms usually base the price on that day's trading session (last settled or average of last trades). Other methods such as using forward curves are also used as basis of computation. In normal manner forward contract matures to delivery. Generally, no contract with any "condition" can be tradable.

The HTP maintains a fiduciary account with a commercial bank which accepts instructions for deposit and withdrawals. All transactions take place via Windows interface enabling user to provide instructions on line.

Trading on the HTP will take place during business days and time at a specified location. Once a match is made electronic "clearing" of trade immediately take place through an escrow account system. At the end of daily session the contract amount for each transaction is adjusted to reflect the latest market price. To implement daily settlement, the facility will make the following determination.

If the adjusted price is above the contracted value the facility will notify the customer to deposit additional money through electronic fund transfer. The requirement must be met within 24 hours. If the adjusted price is below the contracted value the customer will be entitled to request withdrawal of the additional fund.

User interface
The HTP cash management service allows customers to deposit funds needed for trade and withdraw excess funds once the account is settled, electronically. The HTP, in contrast to the older settlement, permits the cycle to be completed online within 24 hours in a given time zone.

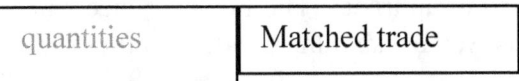

| quantities | Matched trade |

The matching process of a trade triggers the following sequences.

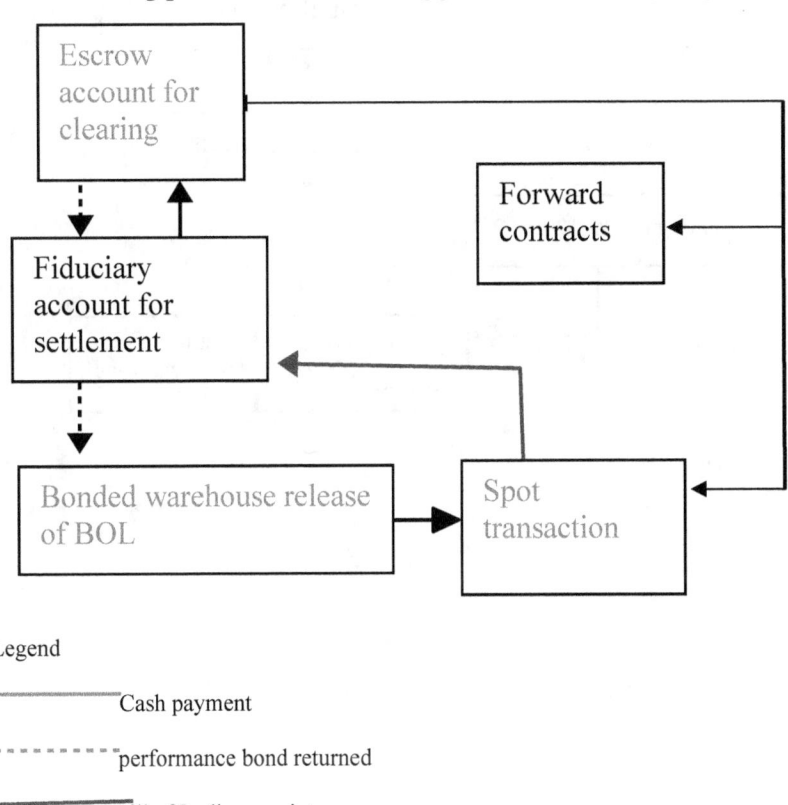

Legend

———————— Cash payment

- - - - - - - - performance bond returned

———————— Bill of Lading receipt

Fig. 1: Matching process for cash against delivery of goods

The built-in "Escrow account", directly linked to the Fiduciary account handles the clearing of all trades. The Fiduciary account manages deposits and withdrawal, as well as handling the daily settlement.

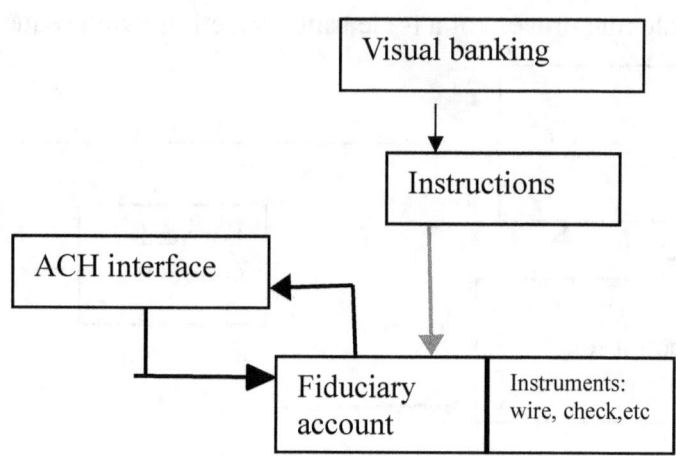

Fig. 2: Deposit flow

The Implementation

The HTP maintains fiduciary accounts at designated(partner)local banks for each Node of operation. The designated local bank provides a conduit for
flow of cash embedded in HTP's financial service. The service functions are outlined below.

- Monitoring payments to fiduciary accounts, including deposits.
- Real-time monitoring of account movement which contain; multi-bank payment & receiving transaction information, including accounts' balance for intra-day and end-of-day held at other customers bank accounts as well as forward balance.
- Historical data will be available on all transactions.
- Standard security features are implemented.

For the nodes located in the U.S.(and Canada) ACH services are available through most commercial banks.

Setting up ACH

A customer creates a payment request providing such information as Participant's Authorization form for payment/deposit includes transit; routing number, Account number and customer's name (or the cancelled check)

- Account number (PIN). This is tagged to the deposited funds.
- Amount to be transferred from customer's account
- method of remittance (ACH)
- date (day and hour) to complete payment

The relevant information about the customer's account is already stored in the HTP databank during the setting up of the user.

The HTP sets up an ACH transaction and sends it to the designated bank by uploading to bank's interface . Test of pre notification may take six days. File delivery takes 1-2 days before next transaction. The bank intimates the HTP in case of a failure in the ACH process. Additional methods of remittance are also available in the US.

Setting up FED-WIRE

A customer creates a payment providing the following information.

73

- Account number (PIN)
- Amount to be transferred from customer's account
- method of remittance (FED-WIRE)
- date to complete payment

The settlement period

The fiduciary account acts as a common settlement account that allows the escrow account to withdraw from or deposit to at any time. The fiduciary account accepts deposits as they are tagged to an individual identifier, i.e., the pin. A two way fund transfer from fiduciary account to an escrow account takes place.

- Instruction from escrow account to fiduciary for blocking funds
- Instruction from escrow to fiduciary for transfer of blocked funds after the match is made
- Instruction from escrow to fiduciary for additional deposit of funds (margin maintenance)
- Instruction from fiduciary to escrow for minimum threshold warning
- Continuous monitoring of fiduciary account and escrow account statements takes place.

It is important to calculate the time elapsed between the time that money is deposited, the match is cleared and clearing the trade. The concept of T(24 hours) requires that the industry to switch from batch processing to real time processing network. At present the security industry is preparing to move from 3-day to single day. See appendix I.

"T" must include the settlement time (corresponding to credit/debit) in addition to the clearing time that occurs between the time that deposited monies has been received and excess money is available to customer.

Transactions Settlement Cycles:
Time needed for deposit to register in the fiduciary account are as follows.
- Off line including check, wire transfer and letter of credit.
  - Within the U.S and Canada (3 to7 working days).
  - Between the US and outside the US (5 to 10 business days).
  - Within others (3 to 10 days).

- Online, where fiduciary accounts are located are much shorter.
- Within the U.S. (T).
- At a non- designated bank (2T).

Time needed for clearing and settlement- starting from funds availability in the fiduciary account.

Time needed to block funds to allow execution (unblocked if GTC or day order),
- within a Node, anywhere(realtime)
- between two Nodes in the US (realtime)

Time needed to clear (*confirm*) matched order.
- The time elapsed for moving money from fiduciary to escrow account;
  - within a center (instantaneous)
  - between two centers in the U.S. (instantaneous)
  - between the center in the U.S. and EU(instantaneous)
  - between the U.S. and the Far East and within designated bank sphere (instantaneous)
  - between centers at other locations (instantaneous)

Time needed to settle account that applies to "marked-to-the-market" showing available fund for withdrawal purpose, also for the expired contract, off-set contract or default contract. The time elapsed to move money from escrow to fiduciary account or vice versa;

- within a Node(T),
- between two Nodes in the U.S. (T),
- between two Nodes in EU and within designating bank sphere(see chapter V on trading futures),
- between the Nodes in the U.S. and EU(chapter V),
- between the U.S. and the Far East and within designating bank sphere (see chapter V),
- between other locations (see chapter V).

For contracts that expire against physical delivery the above procedure applies. For open contracts the procedure known as Marked-to-market(see chapter I) determines the maintenance margin on daily basis. This will effectively define the "settled" account once the above mentioned adjustments are made. The final stage settlement allows withdrawal of unblocked funds from fiduciary account

The physical delivery module
The nature of the warehouse-The purpose of setting up a warehouse is to guarantee the availability of the goods sold on computer screen. Most spot trades require immediate deliveries and it will be necessary to have the goods ready for shipment before the trade has taken place. To do so, the warehouse must operate as a collection area awaiting dispatch instructions. The instructions transmitted from the clearinghouse include title clearing and the exact point of destination. For the overseas suppliers an additional function of custom clearance must be performed to allow the release of the goods. The bonding, provided by the supplier, is generally used for this purpose.

Since a majority of commodities are repetitive and well established commodities we do not expect any complexity in streamlining the procedure for releasing goods. The physical size of the warehouse will naturally depend on the volume of trade. It also depends on the number of days needed for product to be sold (maximum 30 days). The vendor's position, as practiced by industry for domestic sale, allows an average of 30-45 day cycle for receiving payment after the shipment is made. For overseas suppliers, cash on delivery in the form of Letter of Credit or wire transfer is required. The Event Notification Facility(ENF) for shipping, in either cases, will ensure that the goods are deposited at the designated bonded warehouse. The vendor is legally protected by not issuing a bill of sale (or bill of lading) until an actual sale (match) is made and confirmed by ENF clearing.

Collection
An approved vendor will routinely deposit the goods intended for sales at HTPs designated warehouses. As an example, vendor A deposits goods in Subic Bay Warehouse, or vendor B deposits at Frankfurt warehouse. Upon warehouse receipt the vendor's new product will be listed; or available quantities of already deposited products are modified. Custom clearing staff will be resident at all designated warehouses. Their responsibility is

to coordinate with the resident inspection team (assuming there is no physical damage or shortage) and issue the appropriate bond for customs clearance. Documentation are generally cleared in electronic data exchange(EDI) format with the Government

Inspection team
In an effort to minimize the rate of reject by the buyer and to guarantee a smooth operation a full-time staff of professional inspectors conduct both physical and random lab test to determine the "grading" of the goods. The physical inspection includes the quantity counts, the packing standard, the ISO 9000 compliance, FCC certificate as well as any unusual physical appearance. The lab test includes performance and bench mark evaluation test as well as compatibility where applicable.

Dispatch
The designated bonded warehouse will, upon receipt of pro forma BOL from ENF will proceed to hand over the goods to buyer or its designated carrier.
- The bonded warehouse is networked to ENF for real time communication including receiving/shipping instructions as well as bill of lading(BOL);
- Repackaging of a lot size is not allowed.

Pricing
The seller's price includes shipping cost from factory to his nearest dispatch center (for example, Taiwan producer ships to Subic Bay). The buyer bid includes pickup from his nearest dispatch (for example, Puget Sound). These prices are so designed that a "virtual shipping" from Subic

Bay to Puget Sound will take place. In this manner, traders need not be concerned with the physical distances from the "node" to "node". To each trader it will appear that the good is picked up from where it had been deposited or vice versa.

The T+1 trading
"statements on 24-hour turnaround is tricky" by Mitch Betts

> "WASHINGTON -A panel of securities industry officials today had just one word for the government's deadline for achieving next-day settlement of trades: unrealistic.

The chairman of the U.S. Securities and Exchange Commission (SEC) has called on the industry to clear and settle all trades within 24 hours -or T+1, which means "trade plus one day"- and to do that by June 2002. It will require a major overhaul of brokerage information systems, which now meet a T+3, or 72-hour, requirement.

In essence, T+1 will force a switch from Wall Street's traditional batch processing systems to a real-time processing network that never crashes (see story). The industry supports the T+1 goal but sees the June 2002 deadline as too ambitious for such a big undertaking.

"So much re-engineering is required that it may be difficult to meet that date," said Dennis Dirks, president and chief operating officer at The Depository Trust Co. in New York, a stocks and bonds clearinghouse.

Patrick Campbell, executive vice president and chief operating officer at The Nasdaq Stock Market Inc., agreed. "We've got to have a date ... or we'll just keep talking. The only good thing about Y2K is that we couldn't change the date. But let's get a date that's reasonable," he said. The Securities' Industry Association has a T+1 committee that will propose a new timetable to the SEC.

Dirks and Campbell spoke at a conference here sponsored by San Francisco-based Advent Software Inc., which makes software for

the securities' industry.The industry is undergoing a tremendous amount of change, with a constant series of rush projects to prepare its information systems for the euro currency, the year 2000 date rollover, online trading, decimal stock prices, extended trading hours and T+1.

An industry survey of 250 securities firms found that they expect to spend a total of $500 million to achieve T+1. But Robert Iati, an analyst at TowerGroup in Needham, Mass., suggested the final cost will be more like $1.5 billion to $2 billion.

Iati said securities firms will need to "bullet-proof" their systems because there won't be much time in the T+1 window for slow systems, down systems, glitches or correcting errors. And speakers said processes now handled by phone or fax will have to be automated to meet the time constraints of T+1."

Possible Scenarios

Three traders have made deposits on line in New York (via ACH), London and Tokyo (via common interface). The New York trader's credit is shown at 10.00 am EST. The trader places order immediately.

If a match is made in the same center (New York) the clearing is made instantaneously and settlement is reported at the end of trading session which is usually at 4 PM local time.

If the match is made at a node in the same region (San Jose), but different center or node the clearing takes place within 24 hours after the match is made(the money is then transferred from one center's fiduciary account to another center's escrow account). Depending on the nature and the status of the transaction (spot or forward) the settlement will follow; it will show the exact cash position of trader by transferring back (if any) funds, from the escrow account at one center to fiduciary account of another center.

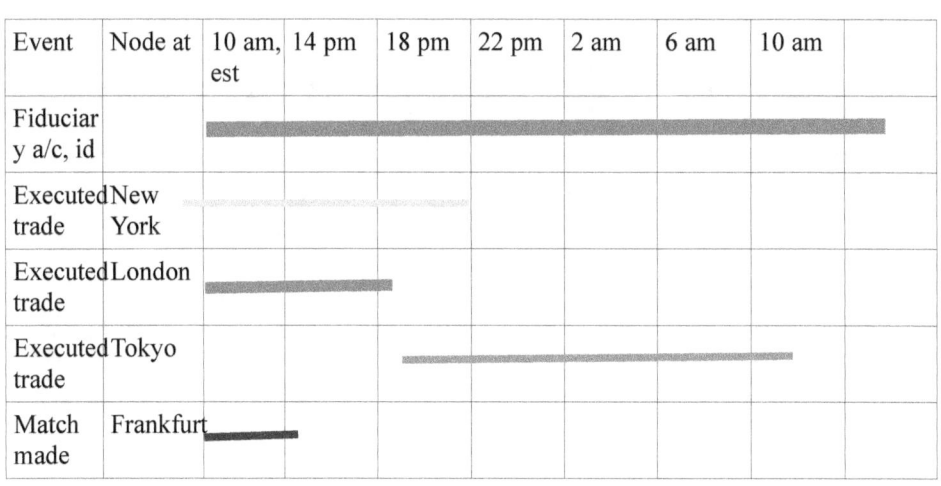

Event	Node at	10 am, est	14 pm	18 pm	22 pm	2 am	6 am	10 am	
Fiduciary a/c, id									
Executed trade	New York								
Executed trade	London								
Executed trade	Tokyo								
Match made	Frankfurt								

PART TWO

Chapter V
A global trading platform

Introduction

A global trading platform envisages establishment of number of trading Nodes at physical locations that identify with producer and or consumer marketplaces related to specific product category or sub- category as tradable listed products. Each node operates autonomously, but they are all interconnected. The products are traded in local currencies in a given node. The inter -nodal trades are executed in US Dollar[1]. All physical product prices are quoted FOB (free on board) at all nodes.

Main components

The Node, or a physical trading center consists of a data-center (cloned in all locations, but with specific data related to the locale); a core support team manages day- to- day operation of the node. The electronic node is Internet based, multi-interfaced trading forum. The operation includes product maintenance, customer relation, logistical support and cash management. Each Node conducts full trading session beginning with front-ended order routing, matching and clearing. The cycle is completed with daily settlement.

The Matching Engine

As discussed in chapters I and III, each Node provides continuous double sided matching locally. The trader, however, has the option to request expanded matching be, i.e., anywhere that another node is operational. All quotes are listed in US dollars in addition to local currency. The physical goods are FOB[2]. In the event a match is made in a non-local node, the corresponding information about logistics and related commerce issues will be available to both parties. Each match will represent a "contract" that one party of a node maintains with another node's party.

The financial clearing

Any order placed at any Node will trigger "blocking" of funds available in the Fiduciary account of the Node. When a match is made the order is executed and the exact amount of performance bond will be kept in the Escrow account. This type of clearing in local currency takes place in real-time followed by daily settlement. For inter-nodal trade, other than the

U.S. the clearing will require a currency conversion which will be fixed at

a specific time of day(such as closing of the local market). There will be a specified amount of U.S. dollar reserve at each node to cover short term fluctuation of currency conversion. The level of maintenance of the US dollar reserve will be dependent on the monthly average fluctuation of local currency with respect to US dollar.

Settlement
At each local Node and at a designated time a batch process for settlement takes place.

- For expired contracts against physical delivery.
- For expired contracts with cash-offset.
- For open contracts marked-to-market and adjustment to performance bond.

All settlement are performed in local currencies.

Currency maintenance
A node will maintain a fiduciary account in the local currency for all participants. At the time of settlement a buyer would normally deposit the required money in the Fiduciary account in the local currency. The converted amount is then deposited in the Fiduciary account to be credited to seller. The conversion rates closely follow inter-bank rates at the time of settlement. An overview of global cash management process flow is depicted in the next two pages.

Commercial Partner banks support users by maintaining Fiduciary accounts for a Node.

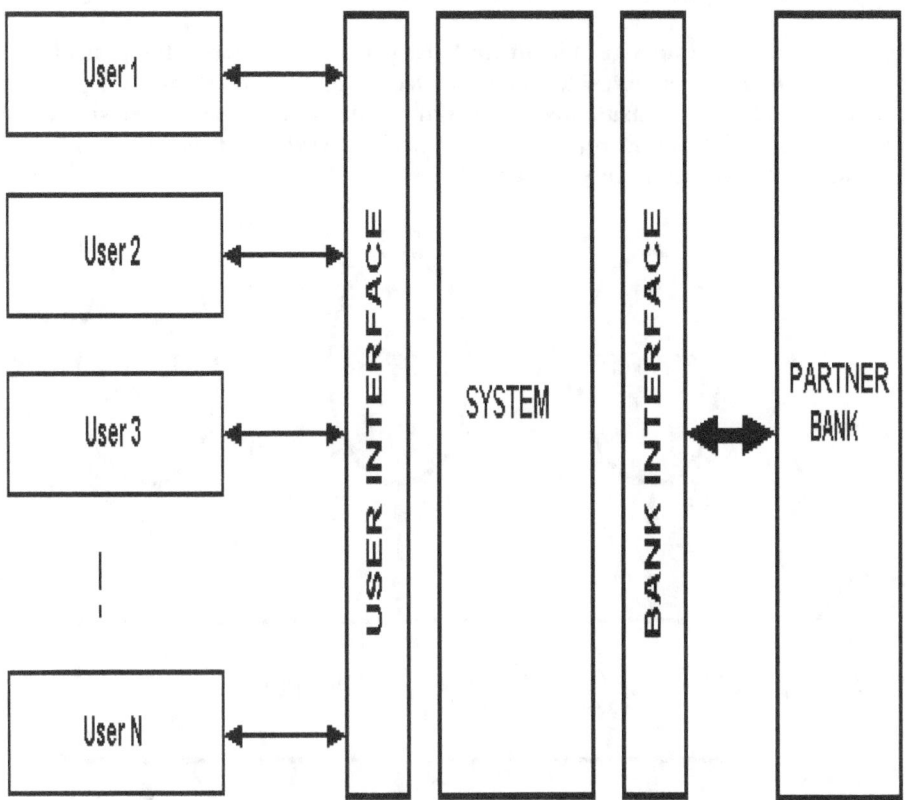

Fig. 1   Node Settlement Process Flow Diagram at Global level is managed through Fiduciary account maintained in Partner bank

The global network of selected nodes is shown below. The locations generally represent the markets where either a large buyer or seller or both drive a particular sector's products. Indigenous marketplace trades in indigenous currency only.

It is worth noting that the size of bandwidth has greatly increased in the past 10 rears. It has jumped from a few tetra bits per second in 2005 to 210 by 2014 according to McKinsey consultants. The major traffic of over tetra bits mostly takes place between the US and Europe and US - Americas. Traffic between US and East Asia ranges from 5-20 tetra bits per second.

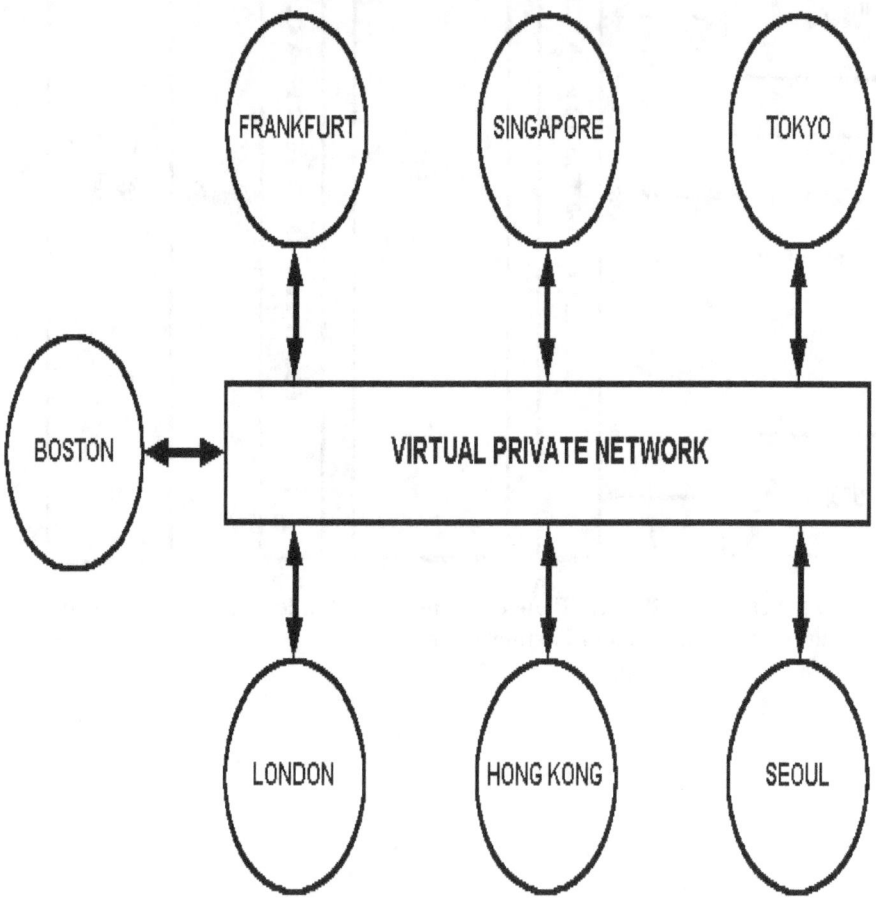

Fig.2: Global Node connectivity

Assumptions and rules for trading members(TM)

Level I refers to single Node.

- There must be an indigenous trading center(Node);
- the marketplace serving local product(s) or market;
- trades are conducted in local currency

Level II

- Regional marketplaces serving multi-markets;
- trades conducted in regional and or local currency;
- all matches, other than local, are made in U.S. dollar

Level III

- For continental trades cross only currencies USD, Euro and JPY allowed

At level II or level III, TM can be a multiple Node member.

Trading in less liquid currency will be available only after a Node has been established in that currency's indigenous marketplace, e.g., Thai currency is available only after a Node is opened in Thailand.

A level II or level III, TM will use the geographically nearest Node as the respective local marketplace and non-resident(NR). Node member follows the indigenous currency or US dollar as the base currency for trading.

The bank account for NR may always be maintained by the TM elsewhere provided the partner bank maintains a branch.

Example of global trade with physical delivery

If a buy order for $20,000 devices with delivery date of 30 days was placed by a seller in mid January, it is expected that a payment of $20,000 be made to seller by mid February . Until such time a performance bond representing, say, 10% of total contract, $2,000 is moved from buyer's Fiduciary account to the Escrow account. This function requires the following steps.

Buyer's deposit of at least one and half times(150%) or $3,000 from his bank to Fiduciary bank account is made. This generally is performed via local banks protocol (in US, ACH).

- Internal transfer from Fiduciary account to Escrow account. This may be done in "virtual" environment without any banking protocol.

In mid February when the delivery is made the entire amount of contract, $20,000 will have to be deposited to Fiduciary account and the performance amount must be returned to buyer. The requirements for buyer are

- buyer's Fiduciary account will be debited $20,000;
- buyer's deposit of $3,000 will be "virtually" re deposited to respective account in Fiduciary.

As for the seller account the performance bond function will be repeated. For the delivery section,

- seller's account within the Fiduciary will be credited $20,000
- seller's deposit of $3,000 will be "virtually" re deposited to his account in Fiduciary

Now assume the buyer is in trading location with different banking protocol from seller's location. Furthermore buyer's location is US dollar based and the seller is in JY denominated environment.

- performance bond deposit function remains the same; buyer's account at Fiduciary is in US Dollar and seller's account in Fiduciary is in JY.

- internal transfer from fiduciary account to Escrow account . This can be done in "virtual" environment without any banking protocol. Each account is in respective currency

In mid February when the delivery is made the entire amount of contract, $20,000 will have to be deposited to Fiduciary account and the

performance amount must be returned to buyer. The requirements are

- buyer's account within the Fiduciary will be debited $20,000;
- buyer's deposit of $3,000 will be "virtually" re-deposited to his account in Fiduciary

As for the seller account the performance bond function will be repeated. For the delivery section of seller's account will be credited as follows.

- US dollar account resides next to JY Fiduciary account
- Inter-bank conversion rate of $ to JY(previous day's close) will be used to move equivalent amount of JY to seller's Fiduciary account.

Note that the amount of $20,000 must first be available in Fiduciary account (buyer). Conversion of that amount to JY will then be conducted through the Node's currency translation

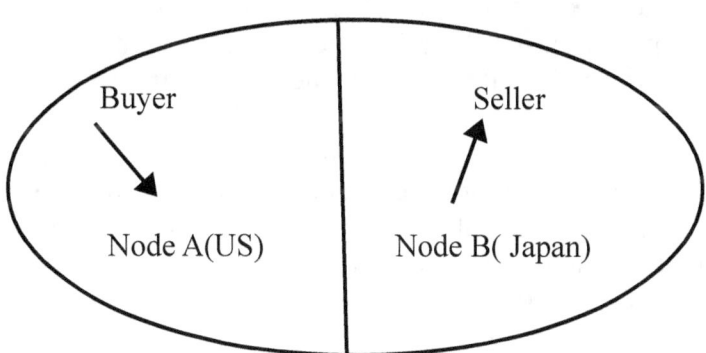

At the time of settlement Node A, after securing the buyer's fund in US dollar from the Fiduciary account sends a message to Node B to proceed and pay the seller out the seller from the reserve Japanese Yen.

If the contract involves forwards, say, 30-day forward; the price may change before delivery. The order to buy or to sell for $20,000 is executed on the basis of 30 day forward price at the date which is match made and cleared, even though it is an open contract, i.e., not expired.

- If the new contract price becomes $22,000 at any time before expiration (based on daily closing of whichever marketplace is higher) it will be necessary to adjust the performance bond. For the difference of $2000 the adjusted performance price from seller will be made in equivalent of JY, using the Node's JY and $ account.
- If the new contract price becomes $18,000, the above step will be repeated, but now the buyer's performance bond in US dollar will have to be adjusted.

Example of non physical delivery

Spot market
The above example in forward rate assumed physical delivery. As the participants multiply and more trades are executed, the spreads between buy and sell prices narrow and the market becomes more efficient. For example, the buyer of the contract at the end of January may decide to sell his contract. Now the remaining period for delivery (when contract expires) is 15 days. This 15 day price, of specified product, at around January 21-22 is $2.88; considered spot price. The new buyer may resell this contract before expiration date if there is a buyer at that time, i.e., high market liquidity exists. As these types of trade increase the differentials between bid and ask shrinks; hence more trade efficiency.

Spot market in multi currency environment
Using the above example, in some cases one side of trade deals with a different currency than US dollar. For the sake of discussion we assume the currency of exchange is Japanese Yen. Starting with an order placed in mid January worth $20,000, these are the events.

- The currency exchange rate at close of the day in Japan in mid January was $1= Yen130 and the equivalent value of order was JY 2,600,000. This means the exchange rate has been assumed fixed at a global rate and without regards to the marketplace. The performance bonds are secured as in previous cases.

Please note that currencies may differ and both traders may utilize non-dollar currencies, but the procedure is the same.

- Assume that the price change of $22,000 occurs before the end of January.
- Seller has now a choice to increase his performance bond as previously described , or
- Sell the contract into the market;

The transaction follows the procedure for the trader in local market.

If the trader is outside the local market the transaction takes the following steps;

        conversion from currency I to US dollar
        settlement remains as previously described

For the purpose of currency adjustments a limited amount of reserve fund in local currency as well as US dollar is maintained at each node.

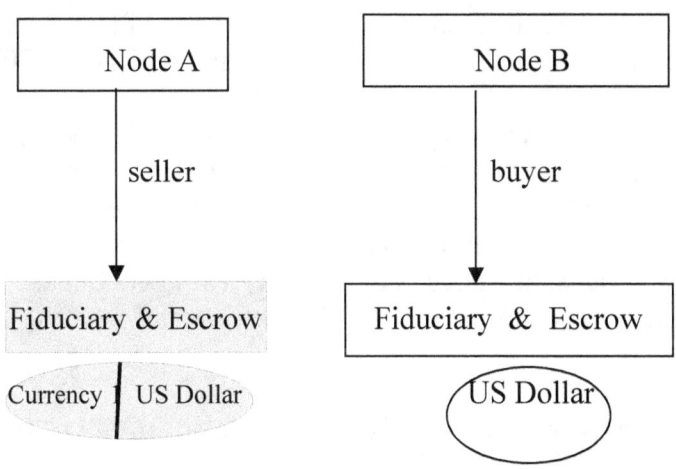

Fig. 3: Process flow of money exchange between Nodes

Assume a contract is sold at Node A. On the day one the contract is worth X in local currency; on the day two the contract is worth Y in local currency. For settlement purpose if X-Y is positive(decrease in value) the buyer needs an additional amount in his currency (US dollar).

- If X-Y is negative (increase in value) the seller adds the needed local currency.
- These additional monies are deposited (via respective Fiduciary accounts) in respective Escrow accounts. The reserved monies of the marketplace will be then used as "maintenance" cost for daily currency fluctuation.
- In the case that buyer is at Node A and seller at Node B the procedure reverses.

Example of cash trade involving foreign currency

Local currency is in Singapore Dollar, the contract is worth $100,000 to buyer in the US and SPD182,000 to the seller in Singapore. It is a 90 day contract and performance bond for each trader is $10,000 and SPD18,200. The local currency reserve at Node A is SPD3,000,000 and USD2,000,000.

If during the life of contract the currency is at SPD1.825 to one US dollar. Then the required SPD500 must be added to the performance bond at Node A, but since the seller at Node A had sold in SPD he is immune to fluctuation. At that instant the marketplace's market-maker will take SP$500 from the reserve account, converts it and adds that to US dollar reserve account. The reserveis now showing SPD2,999,500 and US$2,000,000.

If the currency had appreciated to SPD181,500 the deficiency of SPD500 would be made by taking equivalent amount from US Dollar reserve and crediting it to local currency account (of buyer's node) as follows.

SPD3,000,000 translated to US$1,999,825

APPENDIX I

The following process flow shows message flow for money transfer.

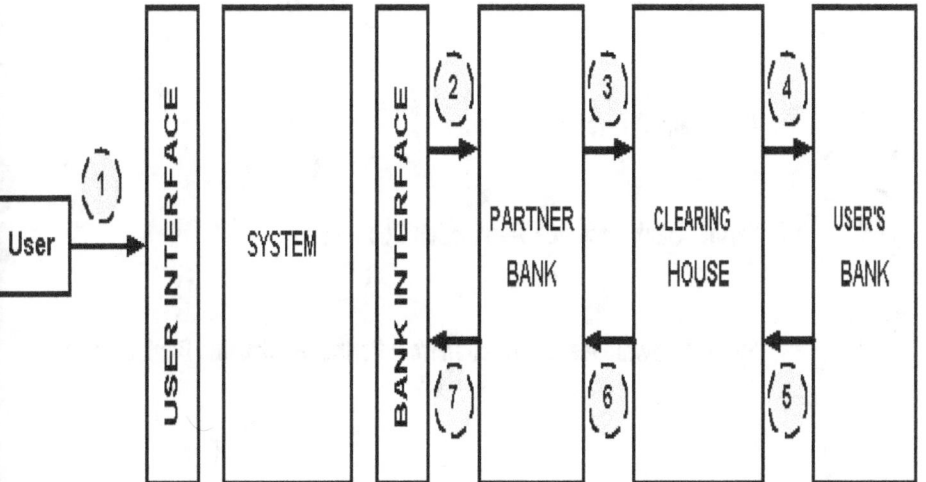

(1)   User Initiates Transaction

(2)   System Uploads Transaction to Partner Bank using Bank Interface

(3)   Partner Bank Trasmits Transaction to Clearing House

(4) & **(5)**   User Bank Clears Transaction

(6)   Partner Bank Receives Transaction Confirmation

(7)   System Downloads Transaction from Partner Bank using Bank Interface

CASE I:

In most cases settlement involves physical delivery and the process flow is shown in sketches on precious page.

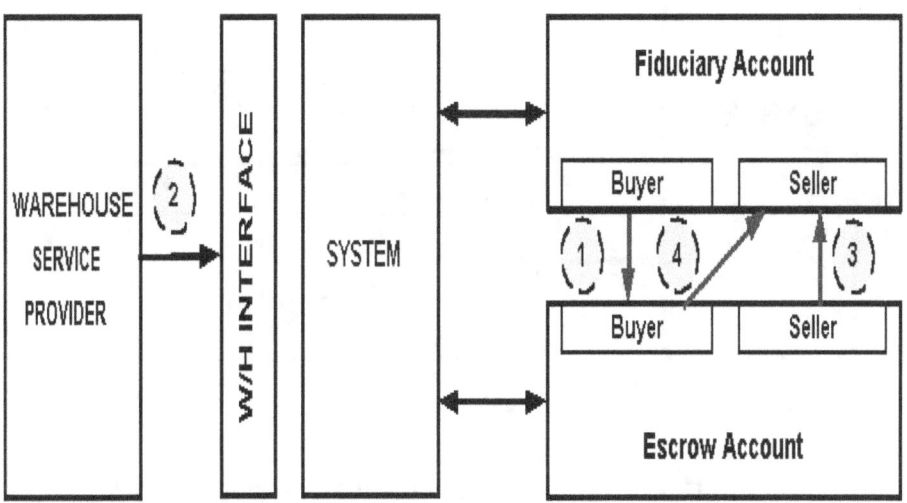

---

(1) **Transfer of Complete Contract Amount**

(2) **Confirmation of Receipt of Goods from Seller**

(3) **Refund of Performance Bond to Seller**

(4) **Transfer of Contract Amount from Buyer to Seller**

CASE II:
In case the physical delivery is replaced (agreed between the parties) by cash offset the flow diagram is as follows.

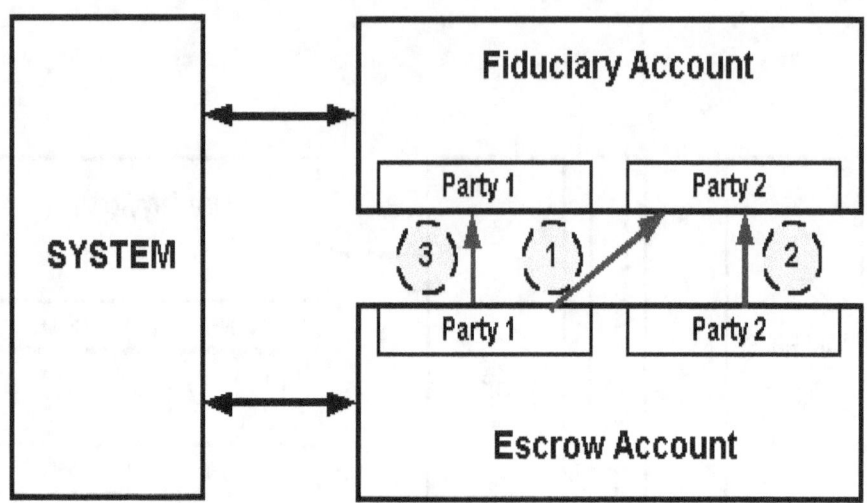

(1) Transfer of Offset Amount from Party 1 to Party 2

(2) Refund of Performance Bond to Party 2

(3) Refund of Balance of Performance Bond to Party 1

APPENDIX II

The Society for Worldwide Interbank Financial Telecommunication (S.W.I.F.T.) is a bank-owned cooperative that international bankers are provided with secured payments messaging services to their financial institutions around the world.

The Trans-European Automated Real-time Gross settlement Express Transfer system (TARGET) is the real-time gross. TARGET was developed to clear cross-border transactions in Europe involving the Euro area. SWIFT has been chosen as the network service provider for TARGET.

Settlement System for the Euro area
The system serves 15 national European RTGS systems that are linked to each other and to the European Central Bank.

Directory Services System and Central Database
Subscribers can send information to the central Directory Services System in order to inform their counter parties. Subscribers can also receive information from other Subscribers via the System. The central System also stores information allowing Subscribers to query.

Information Service Message
The protocol MT 293 is exchanged between Subscribers and the System. The MT 293 is an envelope message intended for application-to-application communication. Information that needs to be forwarded to non-subscribers is sent in the form of a textual MT 999. Only Correspondent_SSI information can be forwarded to non-subscribers. Institutions receiving an MT 999 can reply directly to the Subscriber as per MT 296 and or MT 996.

Directory Services Application
The Directory Services Application is a
software application which allows Subscribers to communicate with the Directory Services System by sending and receiving MT 293's through a S.W.I.F.T. FIN interface. Subscribers can store and access information stored on the Application, and they can export information received to

other internal applications or databases. The use of this Application is optional. Subscribers can enhance their own applications to directly generate and process MT 293s. This infrastructure is available for subscribers to the Treasury Directory and Payments Directory. Subscribers to the BIC Directory and BIC Database Plus will also be able to use this infrastructure in the future. As such, BIC and BIC Database Plus information is sent to subscribers via secured cloud storage , and can be uploaded into the Directory Services Application or into local databases.

APPENDIX III

Currency transaction volume

Trade activity	1995	1996	1997
Cash (spot)	$ 520 million	$580 million	$600 mill
Forwards	$ 670 million	$720 million	$770 mill
Futures	$ 48 million	$50 million	$54 mill

US Dollar Index 2002

Currency	$ Billion	As percentage
$ versus Euro	700	50
$ versus JPY	300	22
$ versus CAD	70	5
$ versus Australia	70	5
British Pound	250	18

Major Contributors 2002

Contributor	Percentage Breakdown	Estimated sectors $Billion
Commerce	45	$550
Travel	35	$430
Central Banks	10	$120

Commerce daily transaction amount

Contributor	Percentage breakdown	$ Billion Contribution
Manufacturing	50	$75 billion
Wholesale distribution	25	$38 billion
Government	10	$15 billion
Others	15	NA

Breakdown of manufacturing and distribution: Size of daily transactions

Manufacturing sector	Percentage contribution	$ Billion contribution
Energy	20	$15
Electronics, components	15	$11.25
Computers/ communication eq	20	$15
Chemical/ pharmaceutical	15	$11.25
Auto/Transport eq.	10	$7.5
Textile	6	$4.5
Metals	4	$3.0
Food	5	$3.75
Others	5	$3.75

PART THREE

Chapter VI
Application of HTP for manufacturing

Introduction
Despite a huge volume and a relentless pace of innovation in the manufacturing sector, the global market in major industrial commodities remains a jumble of inefficient sales and purchasing channels. Poor information, entrenched relationships, costly travel and needless paperwork regularly lead to inflated costs, dramatic price swings, significant transaction risk and a high degree of uncertainty about product price, quality, availability and delivery. Even though there have been rapid gains in productivity in most aspects of manufacturing due to advances in technology and management techniques, the buying and selling processes generally lags because the modern tools for controlling risk is largely absent.

Integrating production and marketing

The classic model of "4 P's" signify the key components of marketing product, promotion, price and place (of distribution) fails to be efficient in a global competitive markets. The global marketing challenges the hierarchical distribution system and redefines the market share. Most important, it amplifies the market uncertainties such as time to market, product shelf life, including the technology age, and cost of raw materials as they change rapidly. These uncertainties collectively contribute to elements of risk, as shown in Sketch X..

A new model may be needed to address the issue of product pricing and its fundamental role in risk management versus the less important P's. To understand how price is the dominant element it is important to consider two distinct product manufacturing models.

Continuous process manufacturing
In recent years' energy sector has shown a definite tilt towards adopting the open market approach to modernize their industries. Since the underlying commodities of these businesses, notably petroleum products and electricity are traded in most exchanges a large and active OTC market participants are able to devise necessary tools to manage their risk efficiently. Recently paper as well as ferrous metals are also traded as futures in major exchanges.

Discrete manufacturing
Specifically electronics sector has only recently been exposed to an informal and sporadic secondary markets the size of which remains relatively small.

On the other hand, many electronic exchanges and business-to- business organizations in recent years are actively pursuing the idea of bringing buyer and seller together electronically. Yet, none would address the issue of open market.

Risk management in manufacturing
Generally, in a business environment there are risk elements that in normal circumstances are assumed to be known among the parties involved in the line of supply chain. Risk management will then help to minimize possible financial losses resulting from price changes. In all these cases formal exchanges facilitate the risk management by allowing the producer and consumer to transfer their business risk to " risk takers". The proposed time sensitive "contracts" can be sold to corporate buyers and sellers as an improved mechanism for risk management. In the past several years it has further extended to some process industries notably, energy and pulp. In all these cases formal exchanges facilitate the risk management by allowing the producer and consumer to transfer their business risk to risk takers. Below is a sketch, demonstrating the concept.

The following sketch is an overview of how risk is quantified and ultimately monetized.

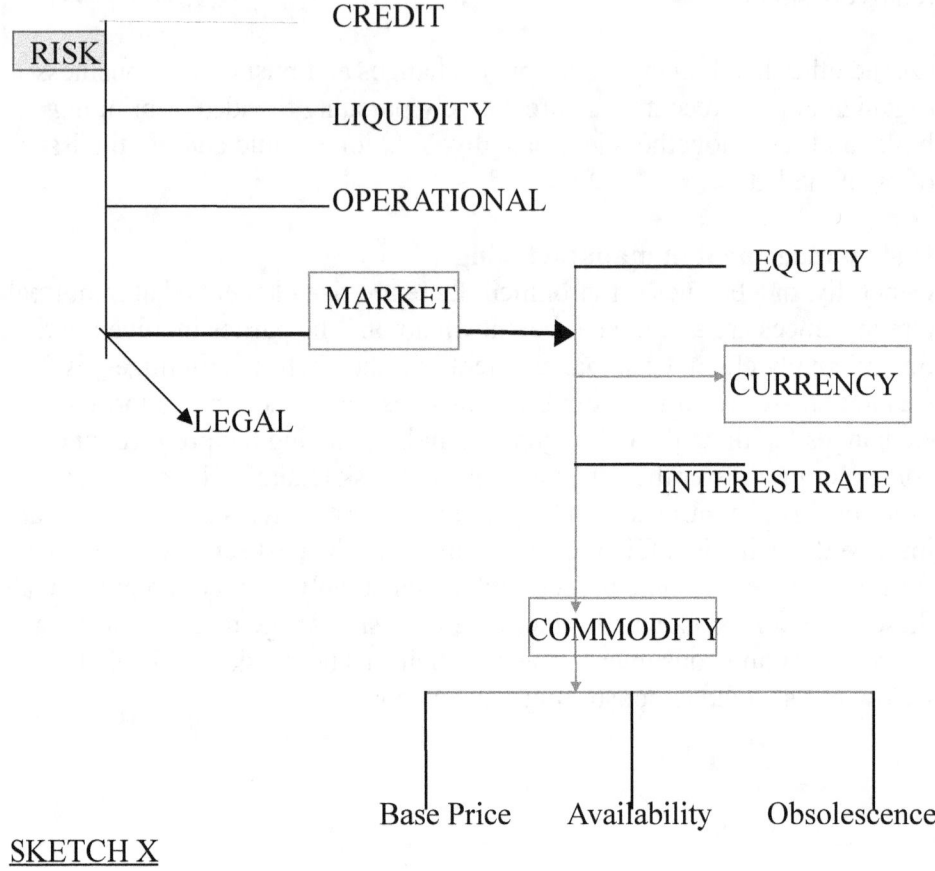

SKETCH X

The sketch X contains elements of risks such as credit, operation,..etc.

One such risk element is the market risk that is subjected to change and hence a variable. The market functions, e.g., as the commoditized products based on their physical properties while the product itself is function of specific variables. So is the currency of trade.

The manufacturing community has not yet addressed the issue of shifting risk which requires moving the product from tangible assets(the inventory) to paper trading. Additionally, minimizing the cost of storage/inventory provides a strong and logical economic justification. The HTP will accommodate the producers' "zero inventory" philosophy very neatly. In summary risk management application in manufacturing;

- ends the boom and bust cycle by creating price stability in basic commodities,
- frees up capital for industry's insatiable appetite,
- lowers the cost to consumer by creating more competitive business.

Key elements of system application

These elements require knowledge of products. Acquiring knowledge of products involves the *selection process* of manufactured products which would, in turn, require *knowledge based* engines that will then provide a methodology for generating products that can be "traded". See chapter III for details.

- Classification of manufacturers parts
- Extraction and compilation of sales figures per product
- Application of 80/20 rule to compute products market share
- Rationalizing products grouping based on the above
- Extraction of technical spec per product category
- Rationalizing manufacturers part numbers based on root specification
- Generating root product's specifications.

Managing risk

The Hybrid Trading Platform, described in chapter I, accommodate the risk management by maintaining daily mark-to-market balanced with automatic adjustment of performance bond.

Physical delivery

The system as described in chapter IV, minimizes the cost of storage and inventory; and provides a strong economic justification, considering the cost of carry alone. For a specific manufacturing sector, which covers both continuous process (e.g., chemical) and discrete (sub-system) device, market readiness is an important issue.

Product's market readiness

The globalization of market economies is creating uncertainties for commerce as well as marketers and distributors. In addition to the usual supply and demand factors, the huge inflows (and outflows) of capital from one market to another create a much larger market swing-as reflected in the currency exchange market-than the predictable seasonal or cyclical changes that occur from time to time. This stems from significant inter-commerce trades that take place routinely. Producers are aware of the risk involved in building up inventory if the market goes soft because an untimely liquidation can be costly. Those who build "on order" assume a similar risk.

- A sudden increase in the price of raw materials may seriously affect the corporate profit.
- A fragmented spot market is evolving. It is an $ 8 billion market, a small percentage of the entire $500 billion (US market).
- A traditional contract market exists among manufacturers.
- The spread (as compared to spot) is large because there is no hedging mechanism in place to narrow it for speculative purposes
- Demand (for such mechanism) is expected to be created due to volatility caused by global nature of the business such as currency exchange movement
- as well as rapid rate of technology development causing shorter window of products "time-to-market"

Minimizing the cost of storage/inventory, however, provides a strong economic justification, considering the cost of carry alone.

SKETCH Y: PRODUCT LIFE CYCLE ~ 18 to 24 MONTHS

Clearing-centric platform
Trading platform with built-in financial clearing system offers the following highlights.

External sources
- Several third party clearing organizations notably Clearing Corporation, CME and NSCC, DTC as well as others may be considered for outsourcing. The Internet services availability may require appropriate security measures and firewalls.
- Most major exchanges have a secured private network "clearing" entity that may also be used as an outsourcing for smaller exchanges such as Option Clearing Corporation.

The HTP clearing/settlement model is based on the participation of a global commercial bank for "common clearing" among several major markets, via commercial bank's ACH (owned by 36 members). Web based interfaces are now available in most major banks to allow back office cash management via the HTP. The requirement is that all trades must be cleared within the marketplace trading cycle(T+1, globally). Settlement takes place between local bank and regional fiduciary account within a given marketplace. The real-time clearing also takes place if transactions occur in two separate marketplaces The fund transfer (settlement) takes place between respective regional fiduciary accounts which are interconnected. If the marketplace to which the match is made and that marketplace is closed at the time of matching the clearing is done through the centralized clearinghouse which acts as temporary or general clearing buffer. Its respective settlement will become effective upon opening of the local marketplace. See Chapter V for more details.

Legal issues and regulatory agencies

US market- Generally, the governmental regulatory agency (CFTC) must clear the regulatory issues of trading of commodities on the Internet.

The HTP status is unique. The products are not yet identified as "financial instruments". Further, our initial trading platform does not fall within the scope of "futures trading". Forwards (similar to currencies) are traded as "unstructured" futures. In practice, they serve the purpose of transferring risk from one party to another. The intent is to provide a flexible contracts with risk management tool (again, similar to currency forwards) that would serve the hedgers. The expectation is that the economic value outweighs any potential regulatory hurdles. This is also helpful to structure swaps and other derivative products that remain outside the scope of regulatory agencies.

EU market - Generally, EU has more receptivity towards Internet and less restrictions on trading especially with already tested in US market. No regulations on currency exchange is anticipated.

Foreign regulatory agencies

> *Japan* - Ministry of Finance will be consulted, but we see little objection since the products are not presently being traded in any local exchanges and currency is freely interchangeable

> *Hong Kong (and Singapore)* - Permission may or may not be required from Securities and Futures Commission. This phase of project will be implemented at a later stage.

> *Other markets*- consultation with currency board for Taiwan, South Korea and Malaysia is required for restrictions on maintaining dollar account and converting local currencies to major currencies

Other considerations

Marketplace's risk exposure
The marketplace may periodically take positions to maintain and report market balance. The average number of contracts that are traded daily may reach as high as 700,000 contracts in a given time. For an average contract price of $1,500 the average daily volume is nearly $1 billion. At worst case we expect taking positions on equivalent of 20% of contracts or $200 million. A reasonable reserve of 5% for clearing exposure will be $10 million.

Market size
The numbers projected in the business model are presently based on the two assumptions.
- Large umber of participants in all disciplines.
- Significant numbers of contracts(products).

The entire world market (of electronics) was estimated to be about $1,500 billion in 2003. This number is based on the following statistics obtained from U.S. Department of Commerce.
- U.S. electronic manufactured products(1998) $500 billion.
- U.S. market share (as NAFTA) in electronics manufacturing sales does not exceed 40%.
- Total contract volume is expected to reach 500 million worth about $750 billion. This will represent about 50% of the world market. This is consistent with present commodity exchange market shares.
- As for the number of users we have assumed 50% of existing Fortune 1000 companies plus some 3000 small to medium size (sales between 25 and 100 million) will be attracted to our marketplace worldwide

The liquidity issue
Spot market spreads are narrow enough now that provides good liquidity. The spill over forwards and later futures will largely be determined based on products' other parameters such as buyer or seller concentration ratio. Considerable discussions are provided on this subject, in chapter I.

Chapter VII
Application of HTP for retail business

Introduction

The commodity markets traditionally served producers as dependable marketplaces where a trading mechanism would transfer their risk, i.e. any fluctuation of price, to risk takers. The new investors mat then secure their position by trading their goods at a desired price. The wholesaler or distributor will equally served by this mechanism as they   pass on the guaranteed prices of goods to retailers who, in turn, would add their cost of shelving and profit to arrive at a stable consumer price. Any price change in the underlying commodity will accordingly is reflected at retail price. In an efficient marketplace a change in supply and demand for the commodity will affect the wholesale price. The wholesaler would accordingly hedge his position to avoid any unwanted risk.

The end user may not be protected against sudden or daily price fluctuation of basic staples, but in the long run a relatively stable and hence predictable price will prevail. A well known example is the gasoline price at the pump stations that is translated to consumer. This price transparency does not necessarily protect the consumer, but is the first step towards design of a mechanism to do just that. An example is given at the end of this chapter.

Marketplaces

The marketplaces generally refer to stages of trading or buying and selling of the goods and services. In the financial industry the securitization of the products are known as secondary market with a much broader depth than the primary markets that may refer to entities that originate their products. From the point of view financial markets the secondary market itself can be further classified in terms of structuring the products as well as the nature of players.

- Market I is a regulated exchange which trades structured products. Participants of such marketplaces are producer, wholesaler, distributor or aggregator who hedge their positions. The cash offset position is used in lieu of physical delivery of goods by investors.
- Market II is an unstructured exchange and least regulated that can trade any contracts. Participants are any trading partners with specific requirement in the form of forward contract; otherwise

known as swaps, that may or may not specify physical delivery. A dealer usually employs an external means, such as structured contracts, for partially managing his risk. A dealer is different from broker because of the of the role dealer plays. Dealer in involved in bi-lateral trade with buyer and or seller; whereas broker takes no risk because price does not enter in the outcome of the transaction.

- Market III is consumers (or end users) market with no price protection because it has no marketplace. The reason is that the volume of trade and hence the cost of investing will inhibit consumers or small retailers to enter the liquid market and take advantage of tools available for price protection. A solution is discussed here that involves the application of HTP as an intermediary platform for any aggregators or distributors and ultimately consumers or end users.

Description of the process flow of swap matching
Referring to Fig 1, since the retail business deals with the minimum inventory and maximum turnover it will be necessary to design the products at the lowest level that would in turn facilitate the matching of large number of smallest contract. At each session the HTP attempts to make maximum number of matches. Any unmatched orders will then be treated as ordinary swaps. In a liquid marketplace, swaps can be traded directly by swaps dealer. If the marketplace is forced to take position(in a less liquid market) the marketplace will "interface" with traders by taking net long or net short position in the nearest futures' month. In the event that the product is traded in, other than HTP, such as futures market the process remains the same.

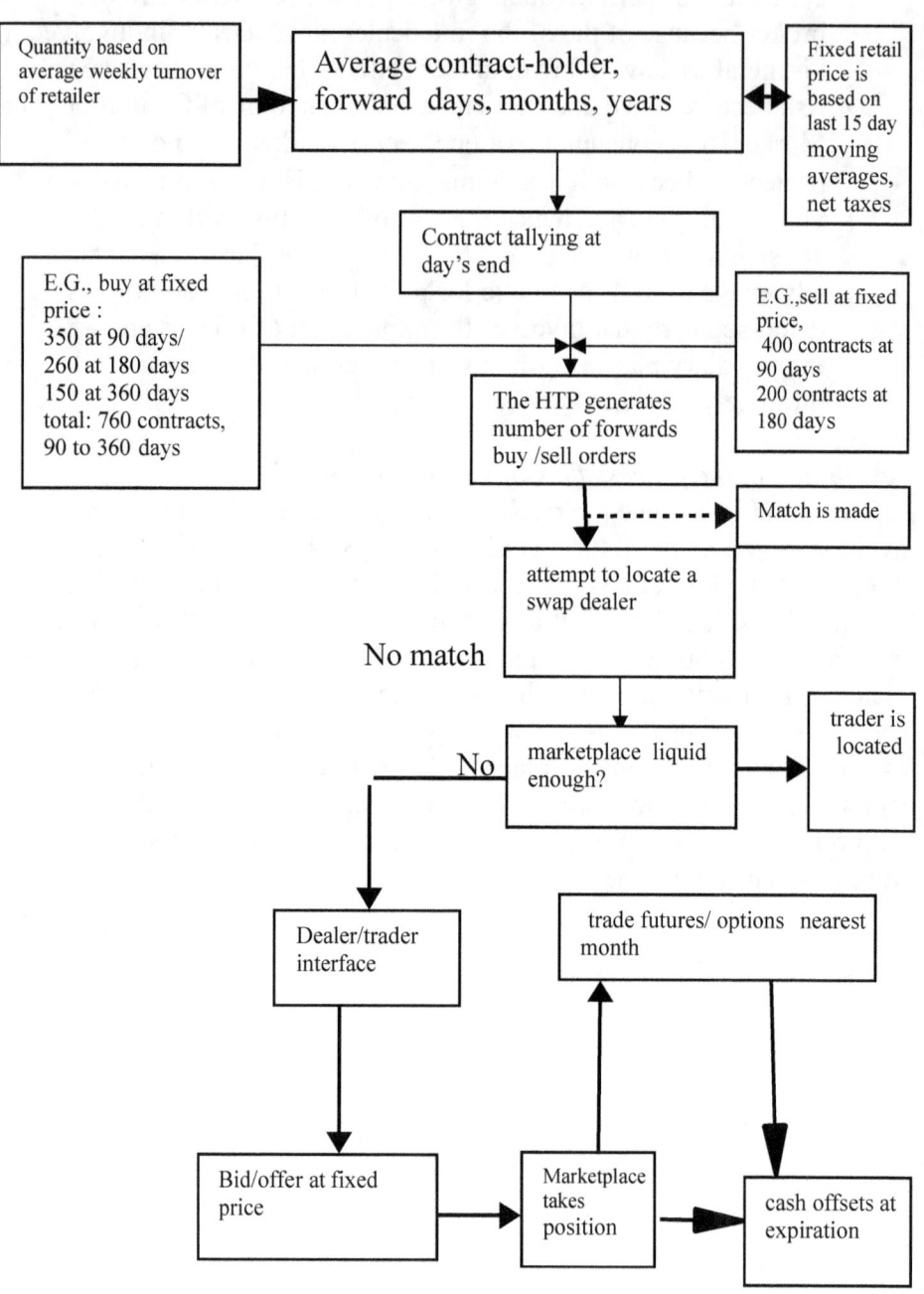

Fig. 1: matching process: Intermediary Platform

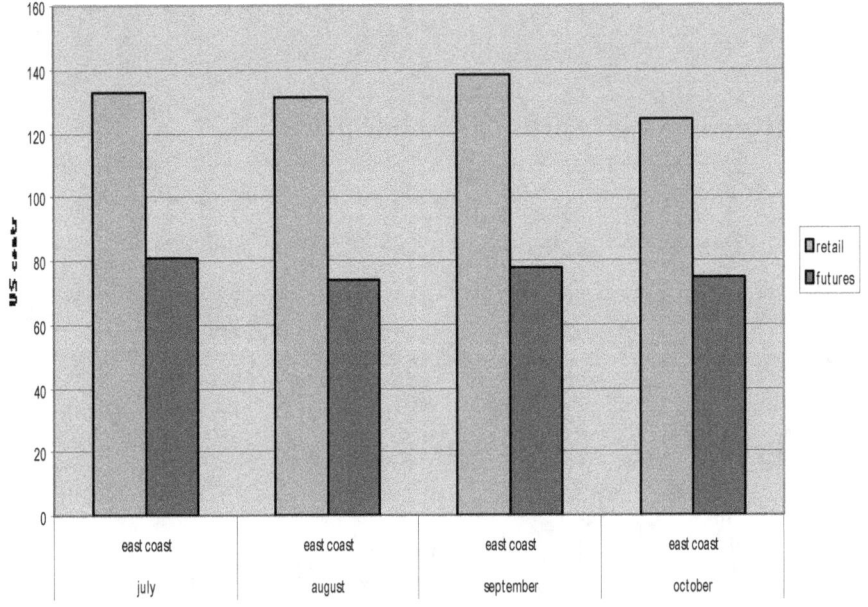

efficiency chart

Fig 2. Monthly price changes of futures and retail(cents per gallon)

Four critical seasonal months: July, August, September and October
Retail prices ranged in the stated months from $1.20 to $1.40; whereas
futures remained basically unchanged in the same period.

As the graph shows the pump price responds to wholesale price at a more
or less fixed delta which means the cost increase will be systematically
passed on to consumer, as seen in Fig.2. Nevertheless, retailers are slow in
posting declined prices,while quick to demand higher price as market.

Fig. 3: Three month forwards of gasoline price

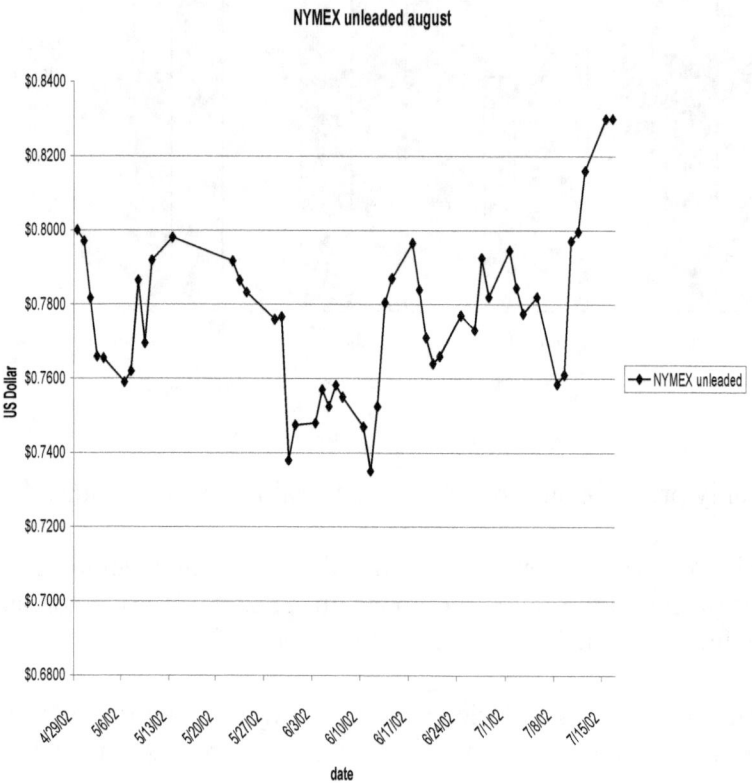

NYMEX unleaded august

This graph demonstrates that during any 3- months season, the price changes would amplify and are more significant.

The end users are forced to absorb any losses by retailer by paying the posted higher price before reflecting any price changes. This is not a two way street. The following example demonstrates a remedy for this unfair position.

Applying the risk management
Here we explore energy products, specifically gasoline. Gasoline changes hand three or four times before being pumped by vehicle user. The pump--ing station owner is also exposed to risk of price rise during the period of lifting, that is, as long as the storage is being utilized. An average vehicle user spends about $2,000 annually. This corresponds to $120 for every 10 cents price change.

An independent gas station owner or franchise holder buys from aggregator without any price protection, hence subject to wholesale price fluctuation. Any increase of price is of course passed on to consumers. Now, the owner of a gas station buys an average of 90,000 gallon a month to fill the station's storage tank. A price drop of 5- cent per gallon translates to $4,500 loss; a sizable part of his gross profit.

The process flow for risk management
Figure 4, shown below, outlines the main events of execution of a derivative contract which contains order processing, matching and clearing. Three scenarios may occur.

Initial matching
At the end of the trade session all orders are collected and processed as buy orders. The orders are show
- Number of lots with each lot size being 7,000 gallons
- Deliveries of 30 and multiple rollover of 30 days
- Price is fixed (market)

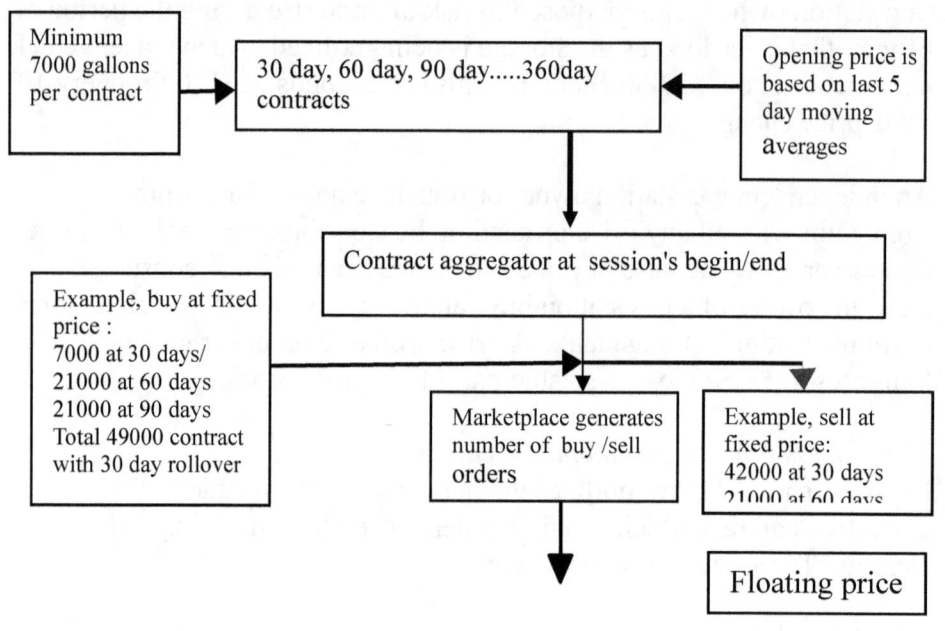

Fig.4: Application of risk management

Dummy matching
After all matches have been made the system will then generate a dummy sell (or buy) order to match most of the remaining orders. The dummy sell/buy prices are derived from 80/20 rule, described in chapter VIII. In this fashion the system acts as a dummy "dealer" accepting those prices that fall within the narrowest range of orders.

Virtual matching
Next, the virtual dealer will then attempt to immediately cover any and all positions.Two sub-scenarios may exist.

- The product and the marketplace is liquid. This implies that a trader is easily available to offset the system's position
- The marketplace is not liquid enough in which case the system performs the following functions
  - It computes the equivalent aggregated matches to arrive at the nearest futures contract
  - It further sorts the deliveries to determine the appropriate calendar delivery of futures
  - It executes buy (or sell) order to create an order as hedge
  - It makes a cash offset at expiration of original contract

Example
Using gasoline as the product three stages are being considered.

Case 1: as shown in figure 4.
> Date: 6-20-02
> Contract: A typical gas station owner has four underground fuel tanks. The most active is the regular gas tank with 8,000 gallons unleaded PRV which is normally filled every 10 days;
> 30 day delivery contract will provide the station with about 30,000 gallons.
>
> Purchased spot price (based on 5 day moving average)is quoted at $0.72/gal. The buy order ($21,600) is fixed upon matching. The present spot price matched is $0.74

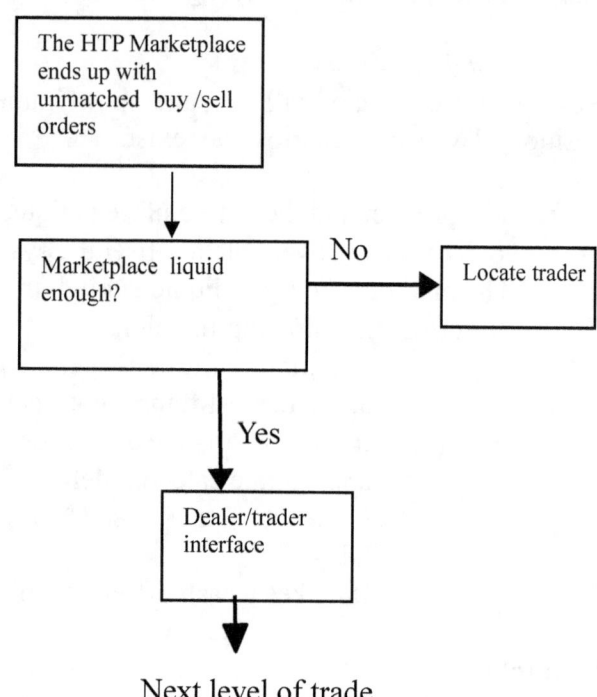

Fig. 5: Swaps opportunity

Case 2, the system has exhausted all possible matches and holds net long or short positions. If the market is liquid the system will merely provide a swap within the marketplace (in the form of bid and ask). If the market is not liquid the system proceeds with the next level of trade. See Fig. 5.

Case 2 of trade history
> Date: 6-20-02
> The system has accumulated orders as following 30 day contracts.
> 420,000 gal., $302,400 buy, and
> 300,000 gal., $303,000 sell.
> Dealer's action: buy 60 contracts with calendar delivery date of July 15 (i.e., October 20th delivery) @ marketplace f.o.b.
> At the expiration date a cash offset by selling the contracts is made.

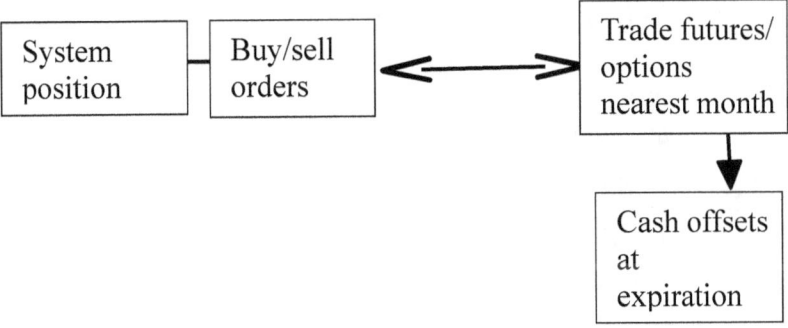

Case 3 of trade follows when there is no match to the above transaction and the market is not liquid (refer to Fig.5) the system will trigger the next cycle of trade.

Using an inter-market interface with NYMEX ACCESS:
Dealer buys 10 futures contracts with calendar delivery date of August and sells, 7 of the same or dealer buys 10 call options with nearest strike price with August expiration date.

Consumer price protection

A solution for consumer's price protection is to "insure" that his cost does not go higher at any given time. This insurance requires mechanism such as option to allow the transfer of risk to take place. The insurance company, who is the insurer, will then be the hedger.

Using the example above, the premium, based on market condition, is assumed to be $ 100 annually, or $30 quarterly. At the end of contract expiration (quarterly) if prices have gone up the market participant would have to send checks to contract holders for the difference using last months (monthly repeated) average prices . So if price at the end of quarter changes the participant accepts LP's average price differential calculated as follows:

Table 1: Forward prices :wholesale compared to the pump
Compiled May 2001

15 day moving average	Crude, WTI, per gallon	Gasoline, unleaded per gallon	
1-May	0.78	1.10	1.70
15-May	0.72	1.00	1.75
1-June	0.67	0.86	1.70
15-June	0.65	0.83	1.69
1-July	0.71	1.00	1.78
15-July	0.74	1.12	1.84
1-August	0.76	0.90	1.75

For detailed explanation refer to the following Appendix .

APPENDIX

Typical storage in a 2-4 pumps- filling station:

Date of contract	5/15/01
Amount contracted	450 gallons
Average national price at the pump for 2nd half May	$1.75
Average national price at the pump for Contract	$1.75
Moving average wholesale price for 2nd half May	$1.00
Difference	na
Average national price at the pump 1st half June	$1.70
Moving average wholesale price for 1st half June	$0.86
Difference	na
Average national price at the pump for 2nd half June	$1.69
Moving average wholesale price for 2nd half June	$0.83
Difference	na
Average national price at the pump for 1st half July	$1.78
Moving average wholesale price for 1st half July	$1.00
Difference 75*0.03 =	$2.25
Average national price at the pump for 2nd half July	$1.84
Moving average wholesale price for 2nd half July	$1.12
Difference 75*0.09=	$6.75
Average national price at the pump for 1st half Aug	$1.75
Moving average wholesale price for 1st half Aug	$1.00
Difference	na
At expiration date, 90 day contract	8/15/01
Moving average wholesale price (last 15 days)	$0.95
Average local price at pump, last 3 month	$1.75
Refunds	$2.25 + $6.75=$9.00

The key data required for continuous collection
Based on the following data, the system will similarly generate orders for
retailers; entering either buy or sell orders in the same fashion.

National average prices at the pumps are available for key periods.
historical (weekly)*; real time (daily); 15-day moving average(regular)
gasoline.
- State-by-state average prices*
- Localized averages per zip code
- State-by-state and other applicable local taxes *
- Daily closing prices, unleaded gasoline NYMEX*
- Premium value for reformulated gasoline*

* denotes availability

PART FOUR

Chapter VIII
Advanced order matching

Introduction

The process of order matching, as previously described, is performed according to the following strategy.

- Upon order entry, if a matching order is found in the system, this part of transaction is closed. Matching is defined as price, quantity and delivery time. No attempt at further processing will be done if the delivery time does not match.

- If the price match occurs but there is a mismatch in the quantity, the user is given the on-line option to modify his order or wait. The user is also shown the available counter offers at the instant with the computer suggested matches defaulted.

- If the price does not match, but the quantity matches, the user is given the on-line option to modify his order or wait. The user is also shown the available counter offers at the instant, with the computer suggested matches defaulted.

- If neither the price nor the quantities can be matched (we also use the principle of pooling to achieve the match and can come up with a composite quantity and price) the user is shown all the counter offers for that product matching the delivery criteria.

- The unmatched order is retained until the end of the business day and then discarded unless the order type is good to cancel (GTC). In case a match is found by the end of the business day, the user is notified by email about the match. For a cancellation, there will be no intimation.

Enhanced matching
Certain steps are needed to improve the efficiency of a marketplace, i.e., the open cry pit versus electronic trading with regards to price discovery. Most matching techniques do not attempt to go beyond simple matching of a single variable, such as price. All other factors remain static. In a marketplace quantity and price are simultaneously announced; the matching is then made by price followed by quantity (partial fill is common). In an outcry pit the price discovery is based on the announced voices at once and without any order. As a result it is difficult to determine the best matched price accurately.

In an electronic forum we may create a snap shot to view all (random) orders and then define criteria for matching. The standard way is to draw supply and demand curve and find the intersection point.The matching price is that point. The matched orders are timed as FIFO. Improvement will be made if ranges become flexible where buyer and seller can define a price whether a bid or ask. The question is then, how the problem of sequencing of orders can be offset against best discovered price. Rapid adjustment of prices would be interpreted as quicker response to new information. This is a measure of external efficiency of the market. The following techniques are extensively employed by most trading houses and exchanges.

Order types
There are two essential types of order; one is user defined, another is based on range and or condition.

Type 1: Limit order (least price trader is willing to trade) has the following properties;

- length of time order is active will be a factor in being effective tool,
- fill or kill order as a special case of stop order (demand liquidity),
- market order (demands liquidity),
- arranging limit order by price to be, start with lowest sell –ascending and highest buy descending (followed by time if market is not open).

Stop order merely sets specific value at which a buy or sell order is triggered. The " type 1" order is used in most trading platforms and is straight forward. The user merely determines the desired market level and the orders are executed accordingly. Limit order to buy normally occurs as " market correction". Limit order to sell, points to lack of price information.

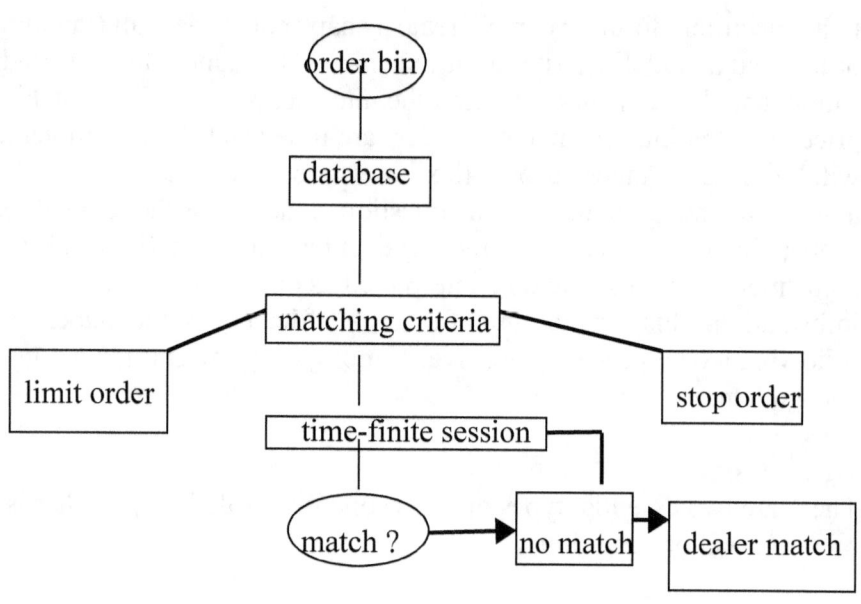

Fig.7- Enhanced Matching engine, Type1.

Designing a range

Type 2 orders are based on negotiation. These are presently off-exchange orders usually handled by dealers rather than traders; these orders are common in OTC products.

@T₁   Session begins

B: bid, O: offer, T: time in seconds for a session

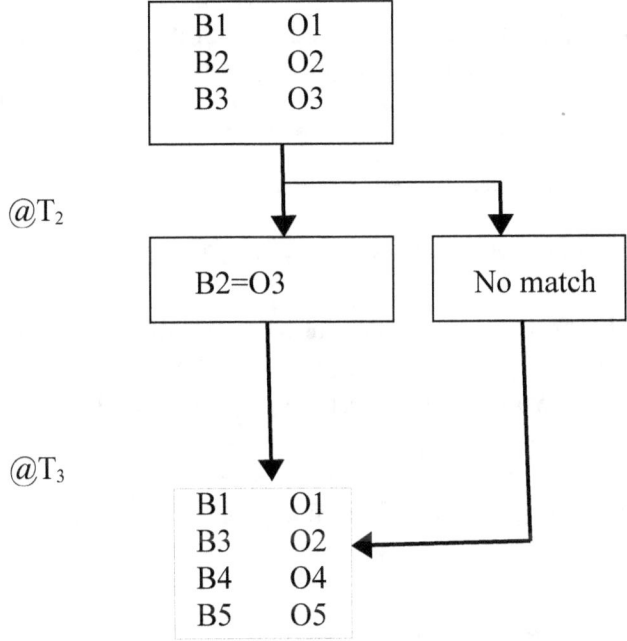

Fig. 2- Matching within specified range

Type 2 orders basically refers to an implied range; it is not user defined and therefore not easily identifiable. Here is a methodology to determine such range.

Averages are generally defined as
- Node
- Mean
- Median
- Standard deviation is a measurement of total variability of the data. It is simply an average of deviations from the mean

Example:
Consider numbers 19   21 21   22   23   25   26   27.
　　　　Mean average=23.
　　　　Standard deviation(SD) = 4+ 2+ 2+ 1 =9/3=3 or (2 +3+ 4)/3 = 3.

In a given distribution bell 80% of bid & ask variation will fall within (+) or (−) x percent of standard deviation, for example, spread of 2 SD, or 4 theta. An application of which would be to determine how many SD will be allowed for best spread.

To determine upper and lower limit, specify how many SD is allowed. These are the steps:
- Calculate the mean.
- Find the range for each period.
- Average the ranges.
- Develop control chart (bid/ask versus time) for relationship to place limit.

Calculate limit for the range. For the market integrity a mathematical model will be needed which will simulate the following parameters.
- Matched orders based on inquiries submitted.
- Number of contracts that would need matching.
- Number of contracts that may default.
- Market makers positions.

Implied price range associated with limit order

If limit order is not accompanied with price range an implied price range will have to be derived. As explained before, in an electronic pit we need to create a snap shot to view all (random) orders and identify all variables as criteria for matching.

Limit orders are then arranged by price, starting with lowest "sell-ascending" and highest "buy-descending". This is followed by the time the order being submitted (after the market is closed). See Table X.

The standard way of drawing supply and demand curve results in finding the intersection point. To do so one may consider a reasonable range in which all bids and asks are listed. We will then try to evaluate the number of bids and asks within the context of 80/20 distribution. That means looking for the relatively few prices being most contested. This approach enhances the standard way of drawing supply and demand curve to locate the intersection point and the matching price will become more flexible within a range; another iteration will of course narrow the range further.

The matched orders are timed as FIFO. This improvement will be made as the range is narrowed enough for market makers. Details of this technique of liquidity improvement are shown in figures 1,2.,3.[1]

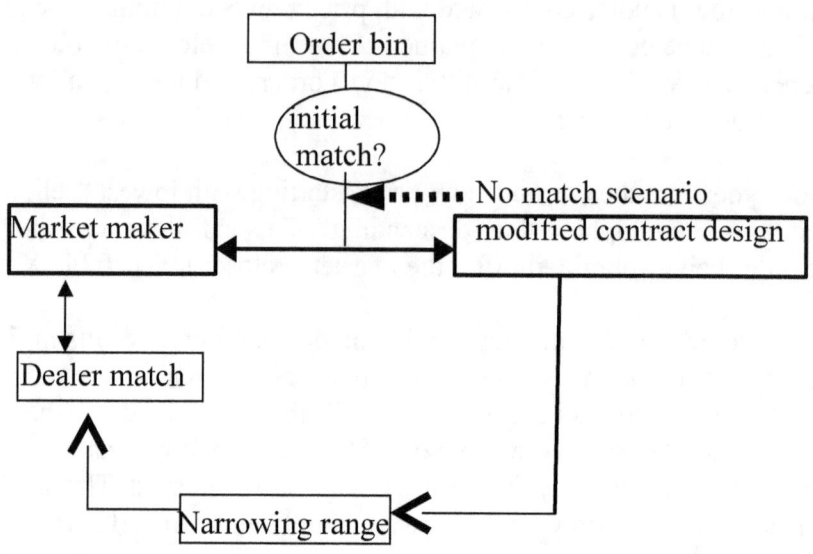

Fig. 3- Narrowing the range

Table X – Arranging limit orders

Number of orders	Buy	Number of orders	Sell
1	5.00	3	5.30
0	5.01	1	5.29
0	5.02	2	5.28
0	5.03	0	5.27
1	5.04	5	5.26
3	5.05	5	5.25
2	5.06	3	5.24
3	5.07	0	5.23
3	5.08	0	5.22
5	5.09	1	5.21
3	5.10	2	5.20
3	5.11	0	5.19
1	5.12	1	5.18
2	5.13	1	5.17
5	5.14	2	5.16
3	5.15	1	5.15
3	5.16	1	5.14
2	5.17	0	5.13
1	5.18	2	5.12
2	5.19	2	5.11
3	5.20	0	5.10
0	5.21	0	5.09
2	5.22	1	5.08
1	5.23	2	5.07
0	5.24	1	5.06
1	5.25	1	5.05
1	5.26	1	5.04
1	5.27	0	5.03
1	5.28	1	5.02
1	5.29	0	5.01
0	5.30	0	5.00

All orders (bid & ask) are counted and tabulated as follows.

- Total bids: 60 ; total asks: 40
- Calculate 80% of all unmatched bid & ask
- Determine the price range
- Do the next iteration in smaller range

Example
1st iteration: between 5.06-5.20 price range there are 45 bids,
second iteration: between 5.15 –5.20,...etc.
Similarly between 5.15-5.30 price range there are 36 asks , and in the next
iteration a price range is adopted, such as 5.18-5.30.

To refine the range further 3rd iteration range should be between 5.15-5.20
Ultimately we arrive at averaging a set of numbers in the narrowest range
possible.

Central Limit Order Book (CLOB)
Most trading houses are localized or, at best, regionalized in a defined
area,where information is shared. The idea of the "central limit order
book" is based on availability of all unmatched limit orders in a given
exchange or trading house to market makers at all times. This implies
interconnectivity among all branches of exchange operating everywhere in
a region[2]. It also requires continuous matching in an electronic trading
forum to ensure that an efficient use of information sharing is made. The
HTP utilizes this concept throughout its trading process by providing the
option for Node operator to request connectivity to any marketplace, that
is, the region open or desired

Chapter IX
Advanced auction

Private auction[1] house

In today's open commerce, private auction houses are designed to dispose of excess inventory, known as direct auction; or to purchase goods, also known as reverse auction. For either of these two possibilities several approaches will be applicable.

- Straight through processing which would involve cash management for taking performance bond as guarantee of match as well as logistics interface. This implies that a private exchange can be used by any corporation
- Ability to switch from direct to reverse at will. This will utilize one auction engine and physical delivery for either or both applications
- Using cash management to guarantee non USD matches and to replace letter of credit.

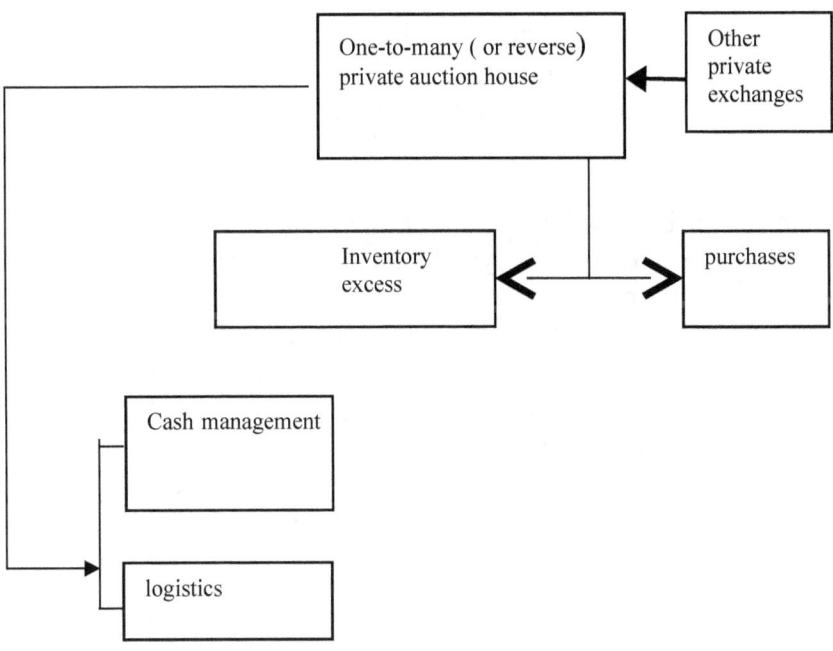

Sketch XX

Matching revisited

A more efficient one- sided auction may be achieved by introducing new methods and tools based on which matching criteria are specified.These are listed below and further presented in sketch XY.

- Fixed price and any delivery.
- Lowest price based on fixed delivery.
- Best match within a designated warehouse.
- Product selection.
- Part number breakdown (applicable to manufacturer as seller or excess inventory holder and buyers for inventory replenishment).
- Tree classification, group, subgroup.
- The manufacturers (database needed for identification).
- Prefix , need to sort and compare manufacturers.
- Suffix , need to sort and compare with product standard or manufacturers' specification.
- Base specification.
- Standard product spec (generically specified)- applicable to general buyer.
- Customer specified, any vendor, general buyer.

Clearing

Performance bond will serve as commitment to execute transaction and no adjustment is anticipated beyond that. The bond value will vary depending on the credit rating of participants.

- o No bond is required if delivery is "spot".
- o in case of direct auction only buyer is required to do so provided the goods are already delivered to a bonded[2] warehouse.
- o performance bond may depend on duration of contract. It will basically be a combination of intrinsic value plus expiration period.

Settlement against physical delivery

Under either auction scenario buyer or seller designates a fixed warehouse. To avoid specific interface for a buyer or seller the common "bonded warehouse" will be appropriate. Any designated delivery locations would then be used as a "leg" to the bonded warehouse. Cash disbursement will also be done through a managed fiduciary account. This will allow impartial and simultaneous release of goods and cash. It will also ensure that the bond is released upon closing of contract.

It should be noted that sorting of unmatched orders will be based on the following criteria

- delivery dates (specified, 30, 60,90, any)
- product group, subgroup, sub-subgroup.

Finer sorting may be necessary if the order was conditional. For example, GLC(good to cancel) or stop order, etc.

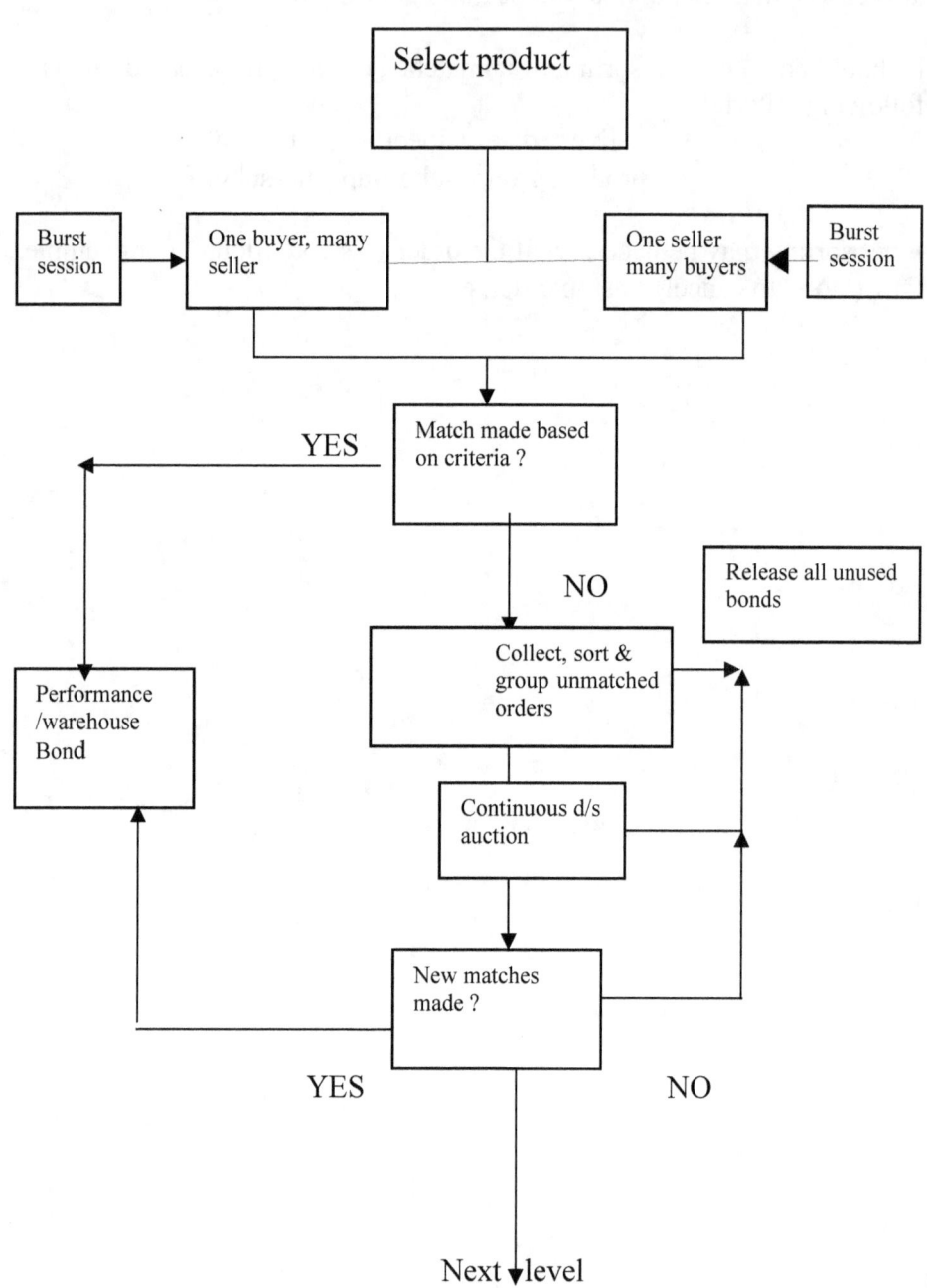

Sketch XY

Example

Referring to sketch YY, a private "auction house" system will be useful to SMITH company. It serves as a gateway to potential parties who are regularly in the look out for the best bid or offer, with whom SMITH had had no previous business dealing.

- If a purchase order is pending it may be placed, according to designated symbol (part number or root of the product), to obtain a match; and if a target price is specified a match may be made accordingly.
- upon identifying the match the marketplace will execute the order by clearing the match and settling the account of both parties through its cash management system.

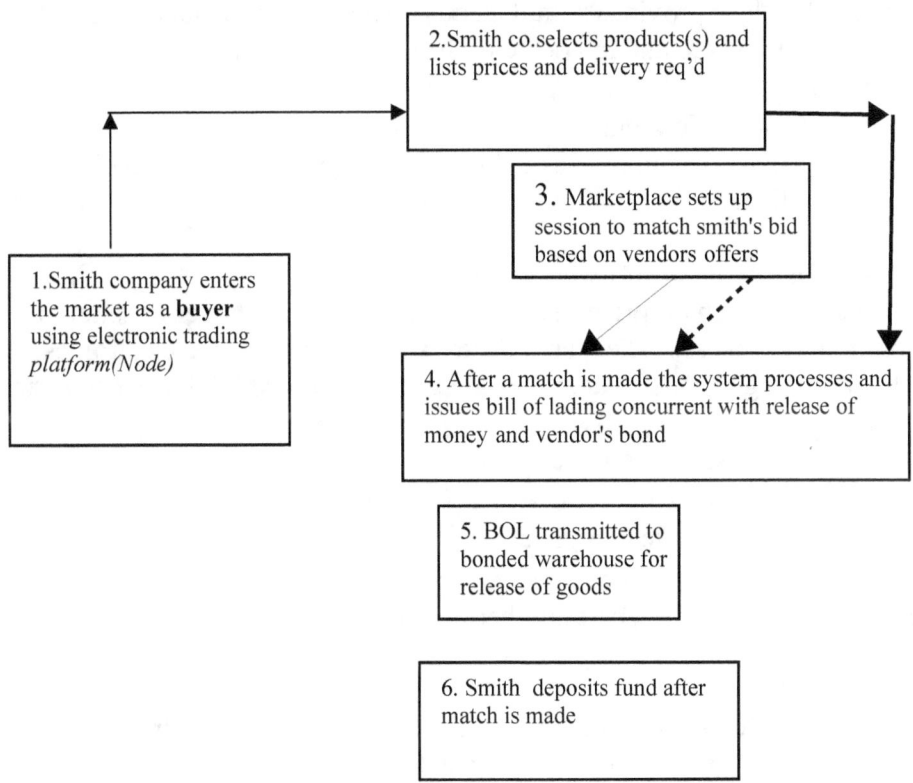

2. Smith co.selects products(s) and lists prices and delivery req'd

3. Marketplace sets up session to match smith's bid based on vendors offers

1. Smith company enters the market as a **buyer** using electronic trading *platform(Node)*

4. After a match is made the system processes and issues bill of lading concurrent with release of money and vendor's bond

5. BOL transmitted to bonded warehouse for release of goods

6. Smith deposits fund after match is made

Sketch YY

135

Explanation of sketch YY
If Smith company desires to enter the marketplace as seller steps 1, 2 and 3 remain the same, but Steps 4 and 5 are switched. That is, Smith must first provide BOL number to bonded warehouse followed by confirmation transmitted to marketplace. The step 4 is now changed to marketplace receiving full cash value from the buyer.

The new step 4 reads: Marketplace fiduciary account, money transfer. The new step 5 reads: Designated bonded warehouse issues bill of lading (BOL) by shipping confirmation. Step 6 is not applicable because for cash market Smith has already provided the goods.

Summary
The marketplace provides simultaneous direct or reverse auction, specifying a session where auction occurs. The system provides
* on-line matching, and
* financial clearing.
A *match* triggers simultaneous delivery and payment for cash market, i.e., cash on delivery.

Order placement for purchase or sale
To place order, enter price(s) and quantities as either buyer or seller; a continuous process. Select an industry sector, for example, electronics. The following products categories are groups from which further selection is made.
* Memory devices
* Logic devices
* Passive components
* Interconnects

For each group enter, a part number or generic product.

Real time payment
When the match is made the buyer of SMITH product has already provided a performance bond. Upon stated delivery date the customer (buyer) will deposit money by wire transfer, EFT or ACH to Marketplace fiduciary account at partner commercial bank . This is accomplished

through Marketplace trading platform. Marketplace's payment system will then disburse money on-line to SMITH on the same day.

In the example outlined above, if SMITH sells 1000 memory devices and the amount is $12,500 SMITH' customer simply deposits that amount in Marketplace fiduciary account thru visual banking before delivery can be made and the process follows automatically.

Physical delivery via designated bonded warehouse
When SMITH buy order is matched, the supplier (seller) will have delivered the products to the designated warehouse . The documentation to support the procedure is done through Marketplace trading platform. On delivery date Marketplace will release the documents to SMITH forwarding agent and SMITH will transfer the fund to fiduciary account for payment to seller. For non-USD transactions Marketplace will provide currency translation.

If SMITH is a buyer and the seller quotes in non dollar currency SMITH will deposit the dollar equivalent of that currency (based on most recent rate and available on screen) to Marketplace fiduciary account at the Designated Bank. Marketplace will disburse money on line to SMITH' supplier in required currency. If SMITH is selling outside the U.S. and the buyer pays in non dollar currency the buyer is instructed to deposit the amount of non dollar currency in Marketplace fiduciary account at (as designated) in major cities. Marketplace then disburses the dollar amount to SMITH on the same day if time zone permits.

Interconnecting private auction houses
Interconnectivity will have obvious advantages such as shared resources.
- Shared resources,
- expanded markets,
- ability to create many-to-many public auction house.

Chapter X
Corporate Financial Projection

Introduction

Considerable money is spent by corporate finance departments as well as numerous research on various forecasting techniques to predict the forward corporate earnings, quarterly and beyond. The issue of unpredictability of operating margin remains illusive. This is mostly because the expected revenue, namely, the price of goods sold, in most cases remain static for a relatively long period. Concurrently the cost of goods is not adjusted for at least a quarter; hence a random operating margin.

Translating the real-time data on prices of goods or their underlying products would provide a basis for computing a range of market price for indexing the cost of the finished goods. This will enable the management to monitor and manage projected level of revenue and production material cost for a given period.

Designing a real time financial projection[1]

A three stage development is required to properly adjust the cost of good, the expected quantities sold and the selling prices. To develop these three stages, it is necessary to identify the key products used as raw materials as well as those sold as finished goods. In so doing, all value-added costs are separated from the cost of finished goods. It is further necessary to monitor the global market positioning of the products, both as raw material and finished good. Last, but not least, market prices for such products must be updated daily, weekly and monthly. A typical process flow of operational design is shown as index II at the end of this chapter.

Stage one

The essentials for product identification in a given manufacturing sector was described in Chapter III. In this chapter we assume a list of such products are readily available.

Stage two

A primary market research is needed upon which real time data can be generated. The real time market research requires the following tasks.

- Market data collection,
- Real-time data analysis,
- A methodology to determine the commonality of key products for a given sector.

For products whose underlying commodities are unknown or lack any international visibility such as cash markets or over-the counter(OTC market) an in-depth research program is needed to create data input. To do so three major functions are needed listed below.

Market intelligence
- Compilation of industry's major players list (company's primary and secondary products and market share).
- Compilation of industry's data for manufacturers (sourced from company's websites). The data include key products, sales figures per product group, and or cost of purchases per group of products(i.e., equipment, MRO, commodity, etc).
- Compilation of shipped products (sources: e-commerce websites and shipping agencies).
- Collection of products price quotes from open markets(HTP)
- Collection of price quotes for currencies (sources: banks or related vendors).
- Collection of corporate financials (company website and Government agencies database).

Stored data
Databases will contain the following fields;
- product (commodity), description, id, industry market-share,
- product (commodity), ID, spot closing with 30-day moving average,
- product (commodity), ID, forwards prices,
- company, ID, commodity1, commodity 2, commodity. 3, sales contribution,
- company's ID, sales, EBIT, regional sales,
- commodity, shipment history, and

- corporate financials filtered for sales (domestic and international), cost of goods sold and earnings.

Processing data;
- computing market shares of commodities and manufacturers,
- computing cash (spot) market size and moving averages,
- computing changes of moving average prices daily, 10-day and monthly for each product,
- computing changes of moving average currency rates daily, 10-day and monthly, and
- computing weekly change of indexes based on "cell" price changes.

Stage III
Index pricing engine is required for developing indexes. Commodity Price Indexes will then be constructed using sound statistical methods and provide a uniform standard (analogous to the S&P 500 for equities and the Lehman Index for bonds) measurement of commodity price volatility. The indexes will be available for use in structuring and pricing derivative products. The consumer price index(CPI) system and proprietary data will allow indexes to be developed for industries presently without indexes. The indexes for non-traded assets will be based on traded products as the underlying financial instrument. Detailed example of creating indexes for semiconductor products are shown in Chapter III.

Accounting implementation
This is summarized below in terms of traditional accounting practices with respect to inventory management. The goal is to transform the existing practices to a "realtime" approximation.

Definitions and accounting terms
The key financial component for a typical non-service company is operating margin. In most cases the operating margin is the variable indicator represented as difference between sales and cost of goods sold.

Cost of goods sold is defined as beginning inventory plus raw material less ending inventory plus labor cost and the indirect cost.

141

The cost of beginning inventory plus the cost of goods acquired, or the cost of the available goods, equals the cost of goods sold plus the cost of ending inventory.

First -in, first-out (FIFO); last-in, first-out (LIFO) refer to inventory movement of goods.

The average FIFO/LIFO costing LIFO tends to produce higher cost of goods(CGS) if prices rise. It is also susceptible to abuse.

Market cost includes write- down and write-off.
- Write-down takes place when the market value is below cost
- Write-off occurs when the goods shelf-life ends or the value of goods is reduced to zero.

Cost of finished good comprises the work-in-process inventory (X) which includes materials, labor, depreciation, plant and services at the end of a period. If the finished goods inventory equals (Y) then the cost of goods sold is (X-Y).

Cost of materials acquired translates to "raw material".

In-process inventory refers to the issued raw materials; plus labor used as well as factory cost at the end of a given period.

Work-in process inventory comprises the cost of finished goods plus in-process inventory at the end of a given period.

Cost of goods sold, shown below is the cost of goods finished less finished goods inventory.

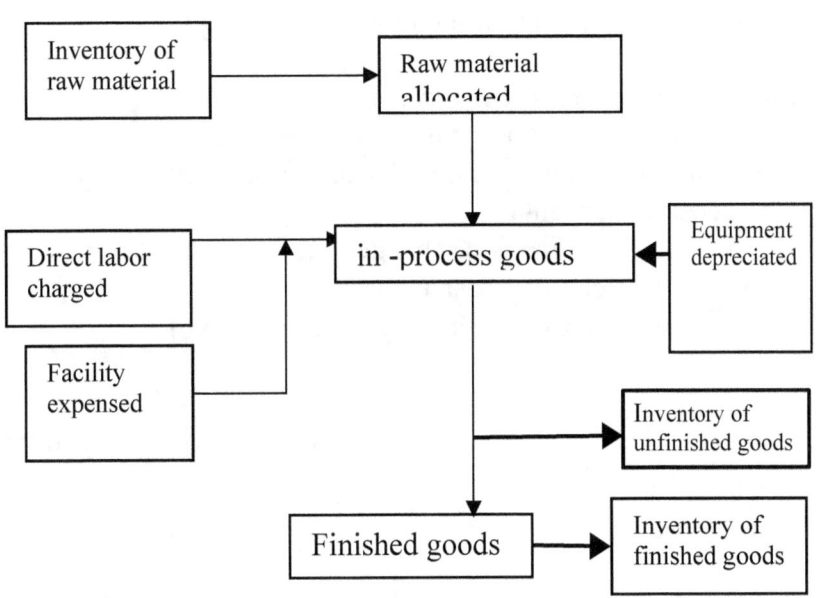

Fig. 1: Process flow for cost of goods sold

Example of, chip maker Intel (extracted from '99, '00 & 1st half of '01)

Average raw material	13% of total inventory
In-process	51%
Finished goods	26%

Inventory/cost of sales	65%

Example of system maker , Sun Microsystem

Raw materials	47%
In-progress & finished	53%
Inventory/cost of sales	47%

Projection

The idea of projecting certain numerical data is presently based on certain assumptions that may or may not to be true. One such example is the assumption that cost of in-process materials and labor is fixed. While the labor cost may be so, but material cost generally a variable. There is also costs related to return of defective goods and or repair as well as consumer products other than those used for manufacturing.

In-process(progress)[2] product costing
- Full costing (long term application)
- Variable or direct costing (short term, based on historical product cost) dependent on
  - resource price change
  - technology change
  - improved efficiency(learning curve)

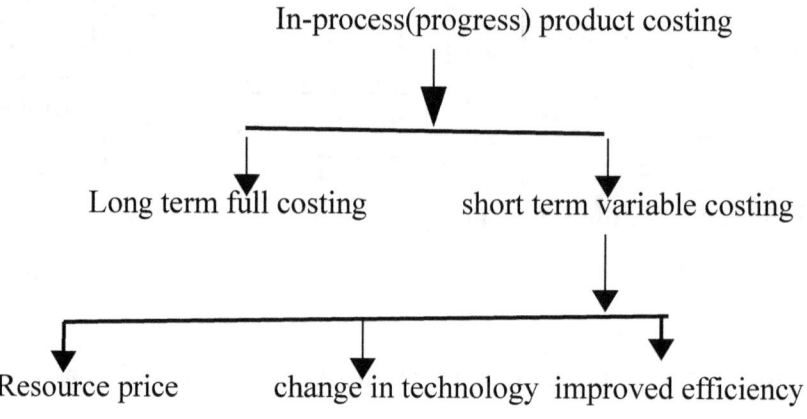

Fig.2: flow of time dependent costing

Inventory components
The existing inventory management systems encompass a comprehensive and wide area and. Every part and or component is accounted for. Under the new approach only production materials are being considered. As shown in the diagram, only those products behaving as commodity products are then analyzed; the assumption being that only those products are market sensitive.

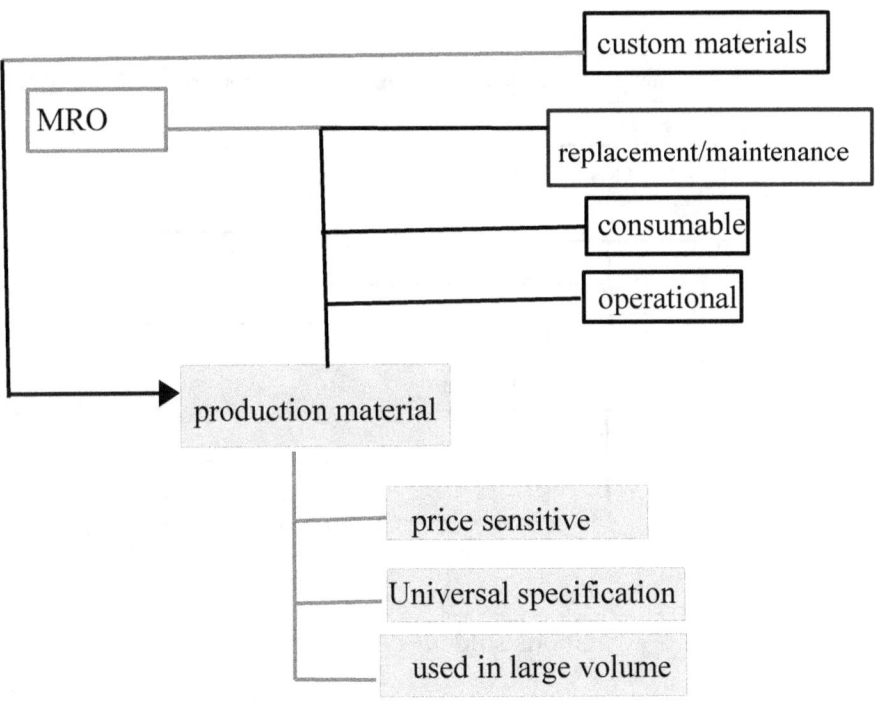

Fig.3: Inventory make-up

Forward pricing

Flow diagram for price change is shown in Fig. 4. The existing procedure is compared with the new procedure, highlighting the step-by-step procedure outlined below.

- define the intervals for which material cost plays part in cost of goods.
- provide pricing data for all such intervals
- provide forward projection, i.e, based on number of days needed for a cycle to be completed

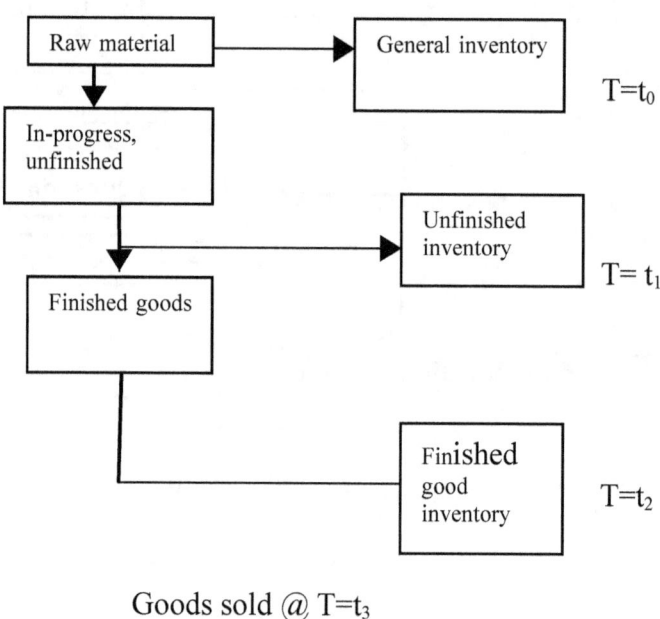

Goods sold @ T=t$_3$

Fig.4- In-process manufacturing flow

A flow diagram of price change

Raw material at $A priced periodically	Allocated for production at $ portion of A based on quantity	Unfinished and finished $portion of A plus fixed for a given period	Goods sold $X for a portion of finished good

P0@T0;   P0@T1for Q1;   P0@T2for Q1=Q2+ Q3;   P0@T3 for Q3<Q2

Under the new scenario prices are updated throughout

Raw materials price paid for goods sold	Allocated quantity price during production cycle	Unfinished and or finished price during production cycle	Price of goods sold during production cycle

$P@T_0$ begins $P_1@T_1$ ends $\underline{P_2@T_2}$ $\underline{P_3@T_3}$

$D1= P-P1$; $P1=P-D1$ $P2= P+D2+D1$ $P3=P+D1+D2+D3$
                 $Q1< or >Q$ $Q1=Q2'+Q3'$ $Q3'< or =Q2'$

Fig.5- inventory changes and real time pricing

Example

50,000 chips were purchased for $100,000 on November 10, 2001 as production commenced by company A

D1= (103,000-100,000), P1= $103,000

During production cycle all 50,000 chips were used to produce 10,000 semi -finished/ finished products which were stored as "finished inventory". In our example, by December 15, 2001, chips prices have significantly increased and the original chips used in the finished goods can now fetch $125,000 ; P2=(100,000-3,000+28,000). For total quantity of 10,000 the unit price of raw material is $12.50

On December 28, 2001 half of these goods were actually sold, the adjusted price was, based on new increase in underlying commodity is then P3=125,000+5,000=130,000, or $13.00/ unit of raw material.

Conclusion
Forward projected cost of goods represents forward projected inventory worth. The inventory's underlying commodity contribution is,
- allocated raw materials for next production cycle,
- inventory of unfinished goods for same production cycle,
- inventory of finished goods for same production cycle all considered unsold.

Forward projected inventory valuation
Market price of inventory of finished and or unfinished goods = material plus standard cost
- finished good inventory = [difference of (raw material @ t_2) less (raw material @ t_1)] assuming standard cost remains fixed
- unfinished good inventory =[difference of (raw material @t_1) less (raw material @t_0)]

If the finished good is traded in open market price is dictated by open market (as memory); if not quantity sold should be adjusted according to cost.

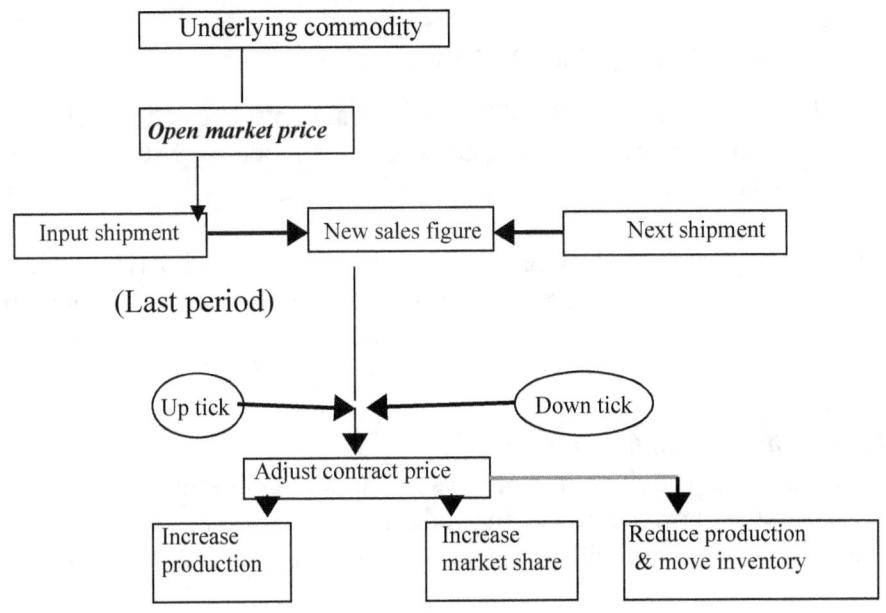

Fig. 6: Open market affecting production and marketing

In an open market, pricing will directly influence next shipment prices as exemplified below. Pricing data are used to calculate weighted average prices through indexing.

In this fashion, estimates at domestic, regional or international levels, sales and delivery data and estimates from other sources will then be greatly enhanced.

Example

Smith company sells products I, II and III:

Week 1: Product I shipped 33,000,000 units at contract price $1.05
Average contract price for aggregate volume shipment is $1.09 (assume 90
day contract). Open market spot price is $1.50

Next 90 day pricing = $1.50 less 0.01 interest. The spread between spot
and forward contract is at present too wide. As this process re-iterates spot
and contract price will converge to a degree.

The benefits to manufacturers
The market data provided by it allows manufacturers to measure the value
at risk for short-term contracts on product price as well as currency. The
processed market data will empower the manufacturer

- to revise product pricing and resulting estimated sales, and
- to adjusted cost of goods sold projections and related financials to
  changing market conditions.

Access to this type of information enables manufactures to re-assess
operating margin on-the-fly. Resulting from such capability are many
opportunities that impact the financial statements.

A longer-range vision of this enables the provision of real time market
pricing data to be utilized in establishing price for non-strategic low cost,
but high market volume items. Dynamic Market Price then becomes a
dependable data point each day. This enables a buyer or seller to update
operating margin on a daily basis. The benefits of continuous updating
the operating margin will instantly influence other departments of
organization, such as purchasing. Other benefits to both buyer and seller
are the reduction of "waste" associated with the current process in place.
These typically consist of negotiating a subjective price for the duration
of the contract followed by re-negotiations and or cancelation of purchase
orders, shipments and de-booking.

Appendix - The Process Flows

The underlying commodity's effect on corporate financials are distinguished in three groups.

Component I defines the mechanics for 80/20 procedure. It begins with a list of products of a group ,e.g., dynamic random access memory from memories that can designate either the production or the finished goods. In either case the dollar amount must accompany each specific item. The amount represents quantity times the unit price.

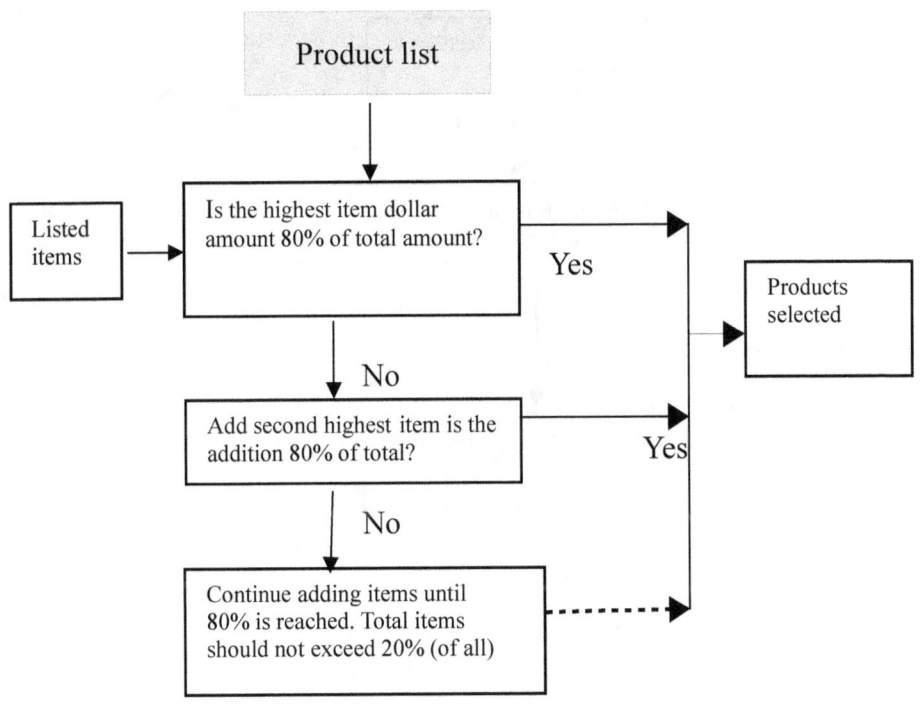

Sketch X: Product selection

Component II lays out the process of product classification for a given group of products.

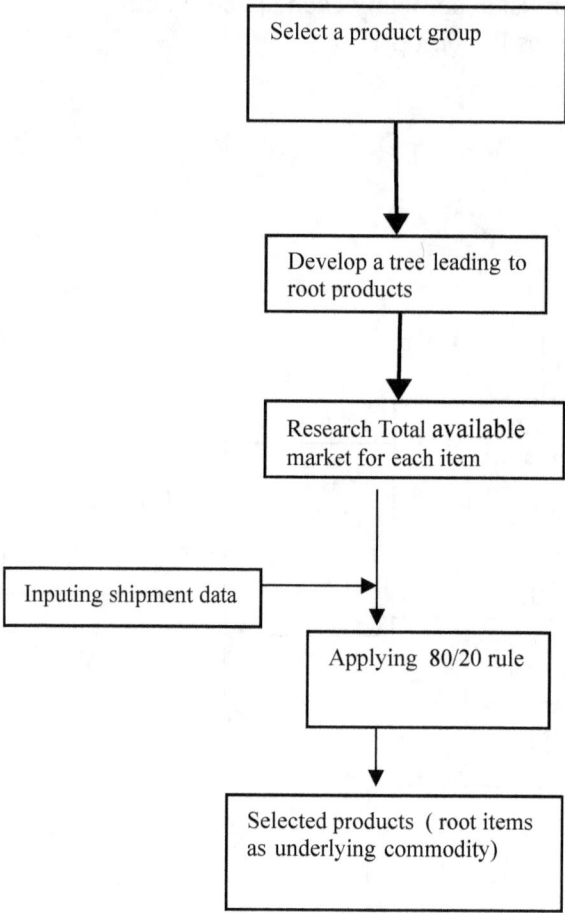

Sketch Y- Exploring root products

Component III – Price indexing refers to building upward the tree to arrive at group index. The purpose, here is to determine price changes taking place between T_1 in base price and T_2. in current price.

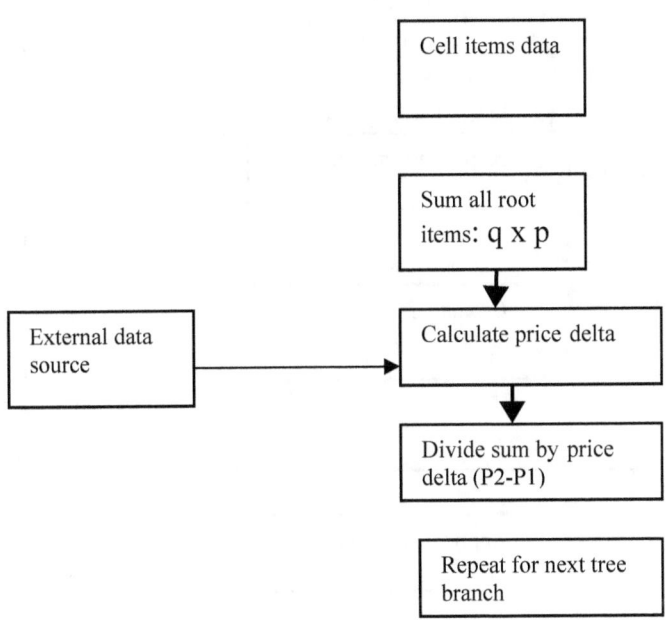

Sketch Z: Index calculation

A system overview

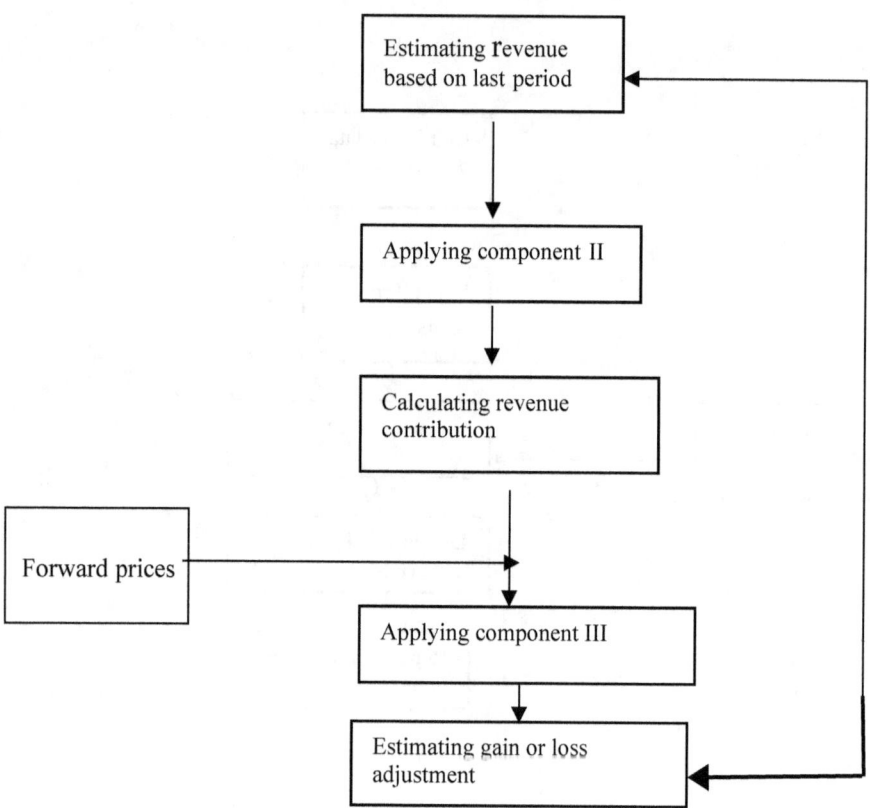

Sketch W: Revenue projection

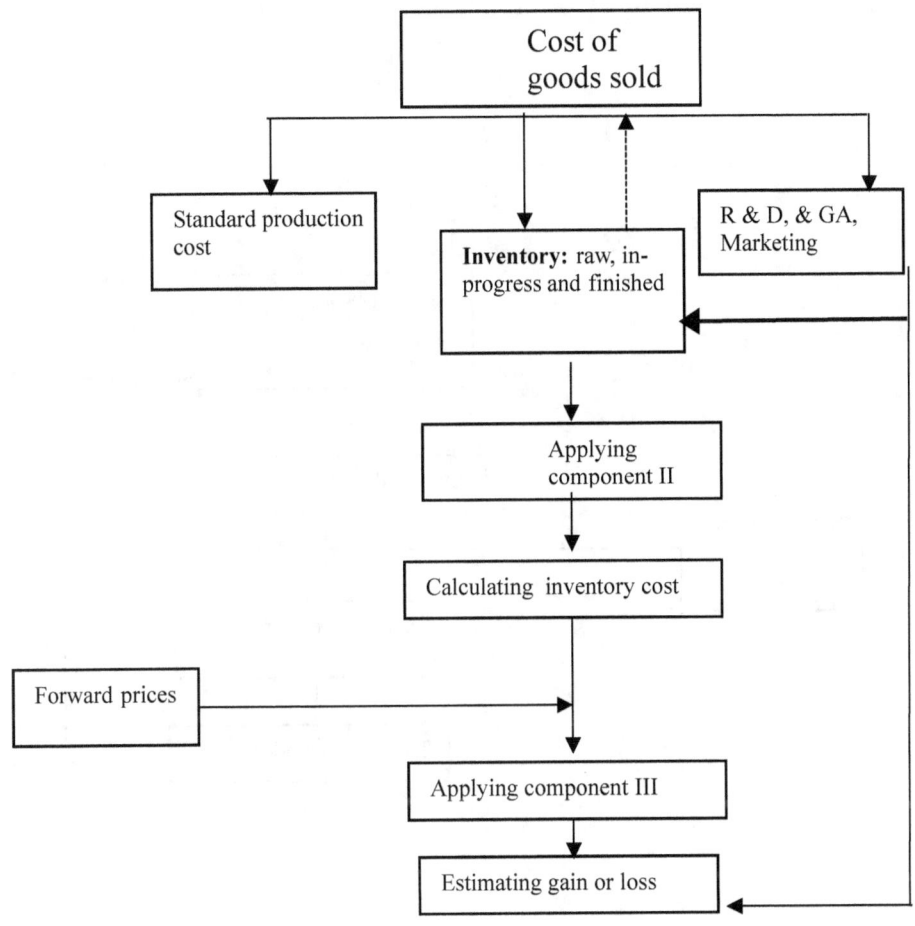

Sketch WX: Inventory costing

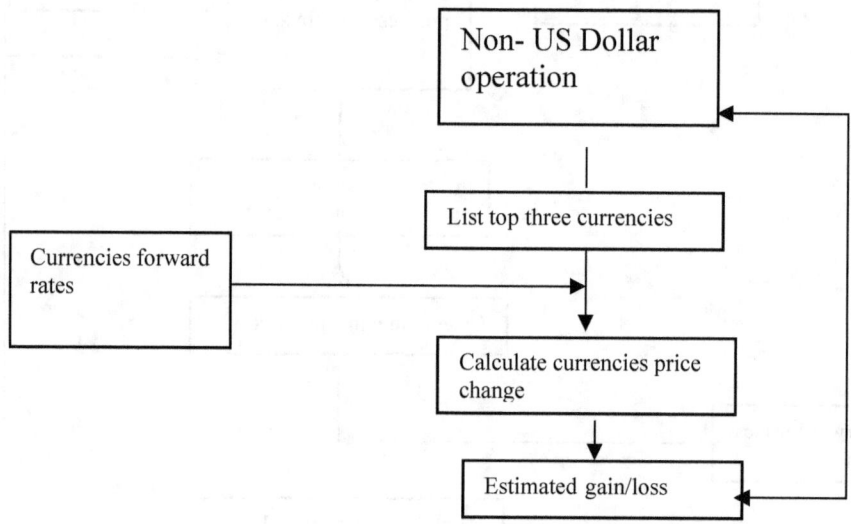

Sketch WY: Currency adjustment

Summary

Stock price is generally depends on supply and demand, market condition as well as "fundamentals" such as earnings and analysts opinion backed up by research. Most research data would be derived from the companies finance division. Most such data are considered "historical". Forward pricing is an attempts to "update" the financial data in real time.

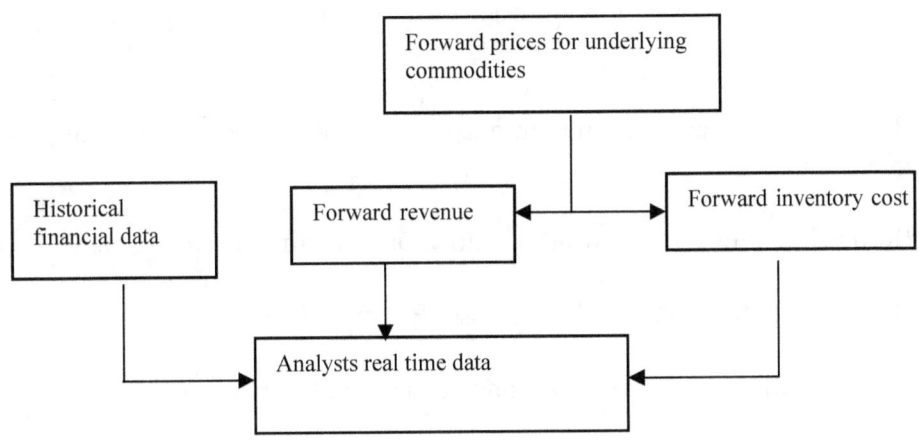

Sketch WZ: The overview

BIBLIOGRAPHY

A) Books

Aggawall,Raj and Lucey, Brian, Forward exchange rate bias and puzzle: Trinity Collge, Dublin;

Alberto Vivanti, Perry Kaufman , Global Equity Investing, 1997

Alexander Lipton, Mathematical Methods of foreign exchange, 2001/2003

Amenc, N and LeSourd,V Portfolio Theory and Performance analysis, 2003

Bhattachya,B. e al.; Causal relationships between stocks and exchange rates, 2003.

Bornstein, Peter L and Aswath Damodaran Investment Management, 1998

Bossaerts, Peter, The paradox of Asset Pricing, 2002

Calvo Guillermo, Money, Exchange and Output, 2006

Clatworthy, Mark Transnational equity analysis, 2005

DeServigny, Arnaud & Renault,Oliver Measuring and Managing Credit Risk , , 2004

Frankel, J.A and Rose, A.K.: Empircal Research on nominal ER

Groppelli, A.A. et al Finance, Barron's 2006

Grossman, G.M. & Rogoff,K.: Handbook of international Economics, Vol III Second edition: 1689-1729

Harrington, Diana, Modern Portfolio Theory and Capital Asset Pricing Model, 1983

Hendry & Nielsen Econometric Modeling, 2007 Princeton publishing Hunt, PJ and Kennedy, JE, Financial Derivatives in theory and practice, , 2004

Krugman, Paul, Exchange Rate Instability 1989

Lhabitant, Francois-Serge Hedge Funds Quantitative Insight, 2004

practical guide to stock portfolio optimization and asset allocation, 1998

Stephen Taylor, Asset Price Dynamics and Prediction, 2005

Zimmermann, Heinz W. Drobetz and P.Oertmann Global Asset Allocation, 2003

B) Journals
Abdialla,I.S.A., Exchange Rate and stock prices interaction in Emerging financial markets, *Journal of Applied Financials Economics*;.(1997)

Ajayi, Richard A. et al. "On the Relationship between Stock Returns and Exchange Rates: Tests of Granger Causality". *Global Finance Journal 9 (1998): 241-51.*

Adler, M. and B. Lehmann. 1983. "Deviations from Purchasing Power Parity in the Long Run," *Journal of Finance*, 38, 1471-87.

Bahmani-Oskooee, M. and A. Sohrabian. "Stock Prices and the Effective Exchange Rate of the Dollar". Applied Economics 24 (1992): 459-64.

Bodnar, G. M. and W. M. Gentry. "The Exchange Rate Exposure and Industry Characteristics: Evidence from Canada, Japan and the US". Journal of International Money and Finance 12 (1993): 29-45.

Chung, S., Young and Crowder, William ,J " Why Are Real Interest Rates are not equalized Internationally?", *Southern Economic Journal 2004*

Courieroux, C and C.Y. Robert , *Journal of Econometric Theory* (Vol.22 issue #6, 2006) Stochastic Unit Root Model

Demirguc-Kunt, A. and R. Levine. "Stock Market Development and Financial Intermediaries: Stylized Facts". World Bank Economic Review

10 (1996): 291-321.

Feenstra, R. and J. Kendall. 1994. "Pass-through of Exchange Rates and Purchasing Power Parity," *NBER Working Paper*, No. 4842.

Ghosh, A. and H. Wolf. 1994. "Pricing in International Markets: Lessons from the Economist," *NBER Working Paper*, No. 4806.

Giovannini, A. 1988. "Exchange Rates and Traded Goods Prices," *Journal of International Economics*, 24, 45-68.

Goldberg, P.K. and M.M. Knetter. 1997. "Goods Prices and Exchange Rates: What Have We Learned?" *Journal of Economic Literature,* XXXV, 1243-1272.

Knetter, M. 1989. "Price Discrimination by U.S. and German Exporters," *American Economic Review*, 79, 198-210.

MacDonald, R:"what determines long and short of it", IMF WP /97121, *Journal of Applied Econometrics*, vol 37, 2006;

Mark, N.C., Exchange Rates and International. (1995) "Exchange Rates and Fundamentals: Evidence on Long-Horizon Predictability" *American Economic Review*, 85, 201-18.

Mark, N.C., and S. Donggyu (2001) "Nominal Exchange Rates and Monetary Fundamentals: Evidence from a Small Post-Bretton Woods Panel" *Journal of International Economics*, 53, 29-52.

Meese, R.A., and K. Rogoff (1983a) "Empirical Exchange Rate Models of the Seventies: Do They Fit Out of Sample?" Journal of International Economics, 14(1/2), 3-24.

Meese, R.A., and A.K. Rose (1990) "Nonlinear, Nonparametric, Nonessential
Exchange Rate Estimation" *American Economic Review*, 80(2), 192-96.

Mussa, M. (1976) "The Exchange Rate, the Balance of Payments and Monetary and Fiscal Policy under a Regime of Controlled Floating" Scandinavian *Journal of Economics*, 78, 229- 248.

Neely, C.J., and L. Sarno, Models of Exchange Rate Determination "How well do Monetary Fundamentals Forecast Exchange Rates?" *Review of Economic Studies, 58, 603- 619 (2002)* Working Papers 2002-007, Federal Reserve Bank of St. Louis

Obstfeld, M., and A.M. Taylor (1997) "Nonlinear Aspects of Goods-Market Arbitrage and Adjustment: Heckscher's Commodity Points Revisited" *Journal of the Japanese International Economies*, 11, 441-479.

O'Connell, P.J.G. (1998) "The Overvaluation of Purchasing Power Parity" *Journal of International Economics*, 44, 1-19.

Rogoff, K. 1996. "The Purchasing Power Parity Puzzle," *Journal of Economic Literature* 34, 2, 647-668.

Roll, R. 1979. "Violations of Purchasing Power Parity and Their Implications for Efficient International Commodity Markets," in M. Sarnat and G.P. Szego eds. *International Finance and Trade* Vol 1, Cambridge, Mass.: Ballinger.

Rossiter, R.D., Ohio University, Term Structure of Forwards Exchange Premiums: Evidence from the 1920's. *Journal of Economic Studies*.2002, vol.29, issue 1, pp33-4

Solnik, B. H. "Stock and Money Variables: The International Evidence". *Financial Analyst Journal, March/April (1984): 69-73.*

Taylor, M.P. (1995) "The Economics of Exchange Rates" *Journal of Economic Literature*, 33, 13-47.

Taylor, M.P., D.A. Peel., and L. Sarno (2001) "Nonlinear Mean Reversion in Real Exchange Rates: Towards a Solution to the Purchasing Power Puzzles" *International Economics*.

C) Other Papers

Carlson, John A. Purdue University; Carol L. Osler Brandeis University September, 2003 JEL classifications: F31, G12, G15 Corresponding author: John A. Carlson Department of Economics School of Management Purdue University, *Currency Risk Premiums: theory and evidence*

Barkoulas, John University of Tennessee, Christopher F. Baum, Boston College, Atreya

Chakraborty Charles River Associates, *Forward Premiums And Market Efficiency: Panel Unit-root Evidence From the Term Structure of Forward Premiums*

Journal of Business and Economics (vol.8 Issue #3, 2008) Evidence of spillover from FX to stocks market

Journal of Econometrics (vol 70, 1996) & (vol. 86, 1998) 337-368, Kuo, B.

Journal of economic studies, Vol 29, issue 1, pp-33-47, 2002

Journal of Business and Economics statistics (vol 61 # 2) 1990?

Journal of Econometrics (vol 70, 1996)

Journal International Economics (vol 14, 1983, 3-24):

Meese, R. and Rogoff, K.

Journal of international Economics, 2000

Open economy models vol. 50, p 117

Open economy inflation, vol. 50, p 185

Oil pricing/prices, vol. 50, p 185 also vol. 51, p 79

Currency transaction cost, vol.52, p 113 PPP puzzle, vol.52, p 321

1. Each product would have a designated *pit* which occupied about 250 square feet within the trading floor. The limitations of physical pit and floor traders are now replaced by computer screens.

1a. ICE now owns the New York Stock Exchange(NYSE)

1b. Financial instrument should not be confused with financial products which refer to specific industry.

1c. related to products being traded as well as the referenced industry, etc.

1d. The author's patents cover the open clearing system and designing tradable products integrated into an electronic trading system.

Chapter II

1. Derivative, in this book, is defined as any tradable products that nay be considered standardized or semi-standard. Standard derivatives are also known as futures and futures options. Semi-standards include forwards that are special type swaps. Derivatives may also come as over-the-counter(OTC) products that cover a wide range of products that may not necessarily be liquid as well as securitized instruments such as insurance-like products.

2.Derivatives, The Wild Beast of Finance, Alfred Steinherr 1998
 Risk Management, Financial Derivative , Saryjit Das, 1998

3. Single platform refers to a reading arena that offers cash market as well as futures or forwards market. This is especially significant for currencies where spot and forwards are not presently traded as forwards.

Chapter III

1.The currency translation is increasingly critical for US multi-national companies as they trade more significantly in foreign countries. As of 2015, according to Wall Street Journal dated February 1, 2016,; Apple,, Microsoft and IBM have reported loss of $5 billion, $1.9 billion and $1.5 billion respectively.

2. g.p. refers to general purpose application

3. specified at 1000 ohm, -55 to 125c, 1/16watt, 50v , continuous rating

4. single in line.

5. The "tsop" pin connectivity is an alternative to dip for memory structure

Chapter V

1. The match may made ,e.g., between nodes located in Japan and South Korea . To avoid any confusion the common currency is USD, maintained throughout the life of contract. Upon final settlement the prices will all revert to local currencies.

2. Free on board is international equivalent of FAS, free along shore

Chapter VIII

1. These diagrams were previously numbered 7,8, 9 respectively.

2. The centralized order limits does not help ant broker or trader who would not be an authorized market member of an exchange or clearinghouse. The fundamental advantage of HTP is its creation of highly distributed trading houses that can access unmatched orders unconditionally.

Chapter IX

1. Definition of auction usually initiates by seller which involves one seller and many buyers. The reverse of this will then switches the participants to one buyer and many

sellers. This latter type of auction forms the basis of wholesale or corporate purchasing.
2. Bonded warehouses are tax-free storage areas that accommodate ports or any temporary locale that facilitates exchange of goods between the parties

Chapter X

1. The public companies generally provide periodic reports on financial health of the company supported by actual numbers. The so called "forward" looking statement accompanying these reports, however, lack any supporting data. Instead there are conjectures or expectation or beliefs that border speculation. Yet, there are reasonable projections that based on certain assumptions charts can be drawn and conclusions may be drawn.

2. Invariably, every physical product needs some "raw" material to change that to an end product; itself becoming another raw material for a possibly system. The term in-process refers to a process in which this transformation takes place.

Index

www.ingramcontent.com/pod-product-compliance
Lightning Source LLC
Chambersburg PA
CBHW070242190526
45169CB00001B/270